THE CANTERBURY TALES

Geoffrey Chaucer

AUTHORED by Robert William
UPDATED AND REVISED by Soman Chainani

COVER DESIGN by Table XI Partners LLC
COVER PHOTO by Olivia Verma and © 2005 GradeSaver, LLC

BOOK DESIGN by Table XI Partners LLC

Published by GradeSaver LLC, www.gradesaver.com

First published in the United States of America by GradeSaver LLC. 2008

GRADESAVER, the GradeSaver logo and the phrase "Getting you the grade
since 1999" are registered trademarks of GradeSaver, LLC

ISBN 978-1-60259-157-8

Printed in the United States of America

For other products and additional information please visit
http://www.gradesaver.com

Table of Contents

Table of Contents

Table of Contents

Biography of Chaucer, Geoffrey (1340-1400)

Before William Shakespeare, Geoffrey Chaucer was the preeminent English poet, and he remains in the top tier of the English canon. He also was the most significant poet to write in Middle English. Chaucer was born in the early 1340s to a fairly rich, well-to-do, though not aristocratic family. His father, John Chaucer, was a vintner and deputy to the king's butler. His family's financial success came from work in the wine and leather businesses, and they had considerable inherited property in London. Little information exists about Chaucer's education, but his writings demonstrate a close familiarity with a number of important books of his contemporaries and of earlier times (such as Boethius's *The Consolation of Philosophy*). Chaucer likely was fluent in several languages, including French, Italian, and Latin. Sons of wealthy London merchants could receive good educations at this time, and there is reason to believe that, if Chaucer did not attend one of the schools on Thames Street near his boyhood home, then he was at least well-educated at home. Certainly his work showcases a passion for reading a huge range of literature, classical and modern.

Chaucer first appears in public records in 1357 as a member of the house of Elizabeth, Countess of Ulster. This was a conventional arrangement in which sons of middle-class households were placed in royal service so that they could obtain a courtly education. Two years later, Chaucer served in the army under Edward III and was captured during an unsuccessful offensive at Reims, although he was later ransomed. Chaucer served under a number of diplomatic missions.

By 1366 Chaucer had married Philippa Pan (daughter of the Flemish Sir Gilles de Roet, called "Paon"--medieval surnames were often changed between generations), who had been in service with the Countess of Ulster. Chaucer married well for his position, for Philippa Chaucer received an annuity from the queen consort of Edward III. Philippa's sister Katherine de Roet (later Lady Swynford, later Duchess of Lancaster) was John of Gaunt's mistress for twenty years before becoming the Duke's wife. Through this connection, John of Gaunt was Chaucer's "kinsman." Chaucer himself secured an annuity as yeoman of the king and was listed as one of the king's esquires.

Chaucer's first published work was *The Book of the Duchess*, a poem of over 1,300 lines, supposed to be an elegy for Blanche, Duchess of Lancaster, addressed to her widower, the Duke. For this first of his important poems, which was published in 1370, Chaucer used the dream-vision form, a genre made popular by the highly influential 13th-century French poem of courtly love, the *Roman de la Rose*, which Chaucer translated into English. Throughout the following decade, Chaucer continued with his diplomatic career, traveling to Italy for negotiations to open a Genoa port to Britain as well as military negotiations with Milan. During his missions to Italy, Chaucer encountered the work of Dante, Petrarch, and Boccaccio, which were later to have profound influence upon his own writing. In 1374 Chaucer was appointed comptroller of the customs and subsidy of wool, skins, and tanned hides for the Port of London, his first position away from the British court. Chaucer's only major work during this period was *House of Fame*, a poem of around 2,000 lines in dream-vision form, which ends so abruptly that some scholars consider it unfinished.

According to Derek Pearsall, "the one biographical fact everyone remembers about Chaucer" is his brush with the law, when, in a deed of May 1st 1380, he is released from culpability in the *raptus* or rape of Cecily Chaumpaigne. No-one knows exactly what the accusation - despite attempts to mistranslate "raptus" as "abduction" - precisely amounted to, still less whether it was rooted in truth. But it casts an ominous shadow over an otherwise pure-white biography, and, rather like the presence of the Pardoner and the Manciple in the Tales, gives a discordant dark wash to our image of Chaucer.

In October 1385, Chaucer was appointed a justice of the peace for Kent, and in August 1386 he became knight of the shire for Kent. Around the time of his wife's death in 1387, Chaucer moved to Greenwich and later to Kent. Changing political circumstances eventually led to Chaucer falling out of favor with the royal court and leaving Parliament, but when Richard II became King of England, Chaucer regained royal favor.

During this period Chaucer used writing primarily as an escape from public life. His works included *Parlement of Foules*, a poem of 699 lines. This work is a dream-vision for St. Valentine's Day that makes use of the myth that each year on that day the birds gather before the goddess Nature to choose their mates. This work was heavily influenced by Boccaccio and Dante.

Chaucer's next work was Troilus and Criseyde, which was influenced by The Consolation of Philosophy, which Chaucer himself translated into English. Chaucer took some the plot of *Troilus* from Boccaccio's *Filostrato*. This 8,000-line rime-royal poem recounts the love story of Troilus, son of the Trojan king Priam, and Criseyde, widowed daughter of the deserter priest Calkas, against the background of the Trojan War. (Compare Shakespeare's version in *Troilus and Cressida*.)

The Canterbury Tales secured Chaucer's literary reputation. It is his great literary accomplishment, a compendium of stories by pilgrims traveling to the shrine of Thomas a Becket in Canterbury. Chaucer introduces each of these pilgrims in vivid, brief sketches in the General Prologue and intersperses the twenty-four tales with short dramatic scenes with lively exchanges. Chaucer did not complete the full plan for the tales, and surviving manuscripts leave some doubt as to the exact order of the tales that remain. However, the work is sufficiently complete to be considered a unified book rather than a collection of unfinished fragments. The Canterbury Tales is a lively mix of a variety of genres told by travelers from all aspects of society. Among the genres included are courtly romance, fabliaux, saint's biography, allegorical tale, beast fable, and medieval sermon.

Information concerning Chaucer's descendants is not fully clear. It is likely that he and Philippa had two sons and two daughters. Thomas Chaucer died in 1400; he was a large landowner and political officeholder, and his daughter, Alice, became Duchess of Suffolk. Little is known about Lewis Chaucer, Geoffrey Chaucer's youngest son. Of Chaucer's two daughters, Elizabeth became a nun, while Agnes was a lady-in-waiting for the coronation of Henry IV in 1399. Public records indicate that Chaucer had no descendants living after the fifteenth century.

About The Canterbury Tales

The Canterbury Tales is at once one of the most famous and most frustrating works of literature ever written. Since its composition in late 1300s, critics have continued to mine new riches from its complex ground, and started new arguments about the text and its interpretation. Chaucer's richly detailed text, so Dryden said, was "God's plenty", and the rich variety of the Tales is partly perhaps the reason for its success. It is both one long narrative (of the pilgrims and their pilgrimage) and an encyclopedia of shorter narratives; it is both one large drama, and a compilation of most literary forms known to medieval literature: romance, fabliau, Breton lay, moral fable, verse romance, beast fable, prayer to the Virgin… and so the list goes on. No single literary genre dominates the Tales. The tales include romantic adventures, fabliaux, saint's biographies, animal fables, religious allegories and even a sermon, and range in tone from pious, moralistic tales to lewd and vulgar sexual farces. More often than not, moreover, the specific tone of the tale is extremely difficult to firmly pin down.

This, indeed, is down to one of the key problems of interpreting the Tales themselves - voice: how do we ever know who is speaking? Because Chaucer, early in the Tales, promises to repeat the exact words and style of each speaker as best he can remember it, there is always a tension between Chaucer and the pilgrim's voice he ventriloquises as he re-tells his tale: even the "Chaucer" who is a character on the pilgrim has a distinct and deliberately unChaucerian voice. Is it the Merchant's voice – and the Merchant's opinion – or Chaucer's? Is it Chaucer the character or Chaucer the writer? If it is Chaucer's, are we supposed to take it at face value, or view it ironically? It is for this reason that, throughout this ClassicNote, a conscious effort has been made to refer to the speaker of each tale (the Merchant, in the Merchant's Tale, for example) as the "narrator", a catch-all term which represents both of, or either one of, Chaucer and the speaker in question.

No-one knows for certain when Chaucer began to write the Tales – the pilgrimage is usually dated 1387, but that date is subject to much scholarly argument – but it is certain that Chaucer wrote some parts of the Tales at different times, and went back and added Tales to the melting pot. The Knight's Tale, for example, was almost certainly written earlier than the Canterbury project as a separate work, and then adapted into the voice of the Knight; and the Second Nun's Tale, as well as probably the Monk's, probably have a similar compositional history.

Chaucer drew from a rich variety of literary sources to create the Tales, though his principal debt is likely to Boccaccio's *Decameron*, in which ten nobles from Florence, to escape the plague, stay in a country villa and amuse each other by each telling tales. Boccaccio likely had a significant influence on Chaucer. The Knight's Tale was an English version of a tale by Boccaccio, while six of Chaucer's tales have possible sources in the Decameron: the Miller's Tale, the Reeve's, the Clerk's, the Merchant's, the Franklin's, and the Shipman's. However, Chaucer's pilgrims to

Canterbury form a wider range of society compared to Boccaccio's elite storytellers, allowing for greater differences in tone and substance.

The text of the Tales itself does not survive complete, but in ten fragments (see 'The texts of the Tales' for further information and specific orders). Due to the fact that there are no links made between these ten fragments in most cases, it is extremely difficult to ascertain precisely in which order Chaucer wanted the tales to be read. This ClassicNote corresponds to the order followed in Larry D. Benson's "Riverside Chaucer", which is undoubtedly the best edition of Chaucer currently available.

Character List

The Host

or "Harry Bailly": The proprietor of the Tabard Inn where the pilgrims to Canterbury stay before beginning their journey. He accompanies the pilgrims on their journey. It is the Host who devised the scheme of the tales, proposing that each tell two tales on the way to Canterbury, and he frequently mediates arguments between pilgrims and suggests who shall tell the next story. He has a bit of a class complex, and can be seen regularly toadying up to the upper-class and higher-status characters.

The Knight

A noble fighter who served in the Crusades. He travels with his son, the Squire. The Knight tells the first tale, a romantic tale of a love triangle between two knights and a woman they both love.

The Squire

A "lusty bachelor" of twenty, the Squire is the son of the Knight, and the only pilgrim other than Chaucer stated as having literary ambitions: he can "wel endite". He tells an interrupted tale concerning the gifts that a mysterious knight brings to the court of Tartary.

The Knight's Yeoman

The Yeoman is the second servant who travels with the Knight. He does not tell a tale.

The Prioress

A delicate, sentimental woman, the Prioress weeps over any small tragedy such as the death of a mouse. She attempts to appear refined, but her refinement is superficial. Her tale concerns the murder of a small child at the hands of Jews who loathe the child for singing about the Virgin Mary.

The Second Nun

The secretary to the Prioress, the Second Nun tells as her tale the biography of Saint Cecilia.

The Monk

A robust and masculine man, the Monk travels with the Prioress and Second Nun.

The Friar (Hubert)

He is an immoral man concerned largely with profit rather than turning men away from sin. His tale is an attack on the wickedness of summoners.

The Merchant

He is an arrogant man obsessed with profit margins. His story is a comic tale concerning an elderly blind man who takes a young wife who proves unfaithful.

The Clerk

The Clerk is a student at Oxford, and his lack of an actual profession leaves him impoverished. Although educated, his intellectual pursuits have left him virtually unemployable. He tells a tale of the humble Griselde, who marries a man of high status who cruelly tests her devotion to him.

The Man of Law

The lawyer tells a religiously inspired tale concerning Constance, a woman who suffers a number of tragedies but is at each turn saved by her devotion to her Christian beliefs.

The Franklin

He travels with the Man of Law. The Franklin is a man who takes delight in all simple pleasures, most prominently culinary ones. His story is that of a woman who promises to have an affair with a man if he can save her husband.

The Weaver

One of the five guildsmen who travel with the pilgrims to Canterbury, the Weaver does not tell a tale.

The Dyer

One of the five guildsmen who travel with the pilgrims to Canterbury, the Dyer does not tell a tale.

The Carpenter

One of the five guildsmen who travel with the pilgrims to Canterbury, he does not tell a tale.

The Tapestry-Maker

One of the five guildsmen who travel with the pilgrims to Canterbury, he does not tell a tale.

The Haberdasher

One of the five guildsmen who travel with the pilgrims to Canterbury, he does not tell a tale.

The Cook

A lewd and vulgar man, the Cook often engages in violent and contentious behavior. He tells a tale that appears to be a fabliau. However, this tale does not exist in a completed form.

The Shipman

He tells the tale of a woman who agrees to have an affair with a monk who will pay her so that she can repay a debt to her husband, but this monk ultimately borrows this money from the husband himself.

The Physician

The Physician tells a tale about a father who, in order to protect his daughter from scoundrels who contrive to rape her, murders his daughter.

The Wife of Bath

The most ostentatious of the travelers, the Wife of Bath has been married five times and is currently searching for another man to marry. The Wife of Bath is opinionated and boisterous, and her tale, which centers around the question "what do women want?," promotes her view that women wish to have authority over men.

The Parson

The Parson is a man devoted to his congregation, decent and principled. His tale is a long dissertation on the definition of sin and its various forms.

The Miller

A large man with an imposing physique, the Miller is rude and contemptuous of his fellow travelers. His tale is a comic story of a devious student who contrives to have an affair with the wife of a dimwitted carpenter.

The Manciple

Also trained in the law, the Manciple tells a fable that attributes the dark appearance and unpleasant sound of crows to the actions of a white crow who told the god Phoebus of his wife's infidelity.

The Reeve

A slender man with a fiery temper, he tells a tale in response to the Miller's Tale. His tale concerns a villainous Miller who is humiliated by two Oxford students.

The Summoner

The profession of the summoner is to issue summons for people to appear in front of the Church court, and in this the Summoner is quite unfair. He tells a tale in response to the Friar's diatribe against summoners that parodies the Friar's profession.

The Pardoner

An effeminate and shamelessly immoral man, the Pardoner is intensely self-loathing yet devoted to his task of defrauding people of their money by making them believe that they have sinned and need to buy pardons. His tale is an allegory about three rioters who find death through their avarice. The Pardoner uses this tale as an attempt to sell pardons to the company, but is silenced by the Host.

The Canon

A mysterious and threatening figure, he and his Yeoman are not original travelers with the pilgrims to Canterbury. They seek out the party when they learn about the tales that they have been telling. When the Canon's Yeoman reveals too much about his master's profession, the Canon suddenly disappears.

The Canon's Yeoman

The assistant to the Canon, he speaks openly about his master's tricks as an alchemist, prompting the Canon to leave the pilgrims. The Yeoman then admits that he regrets the deceptions of his master, and tells a tale that details the methods of a canon's fraud.

Arcite

Theban knight who is imprisoned in Athens but released on the intervention of his friend Pirithous, he and his friend Palamon both fall in love with Emelye. He prays to Mars for aid in his duel with Palamon for Emelye, and although he wins the battle, he suddenly is killed in an earthquake upon his victory.

Palamon

Theban knight who is imprisoned in Athens. Both he and Arcite fall in love with Emelye. Before the duel for her hand in marriage, Palamon prays to Venus, the goddess of love, to win Emelye as a wife. Although he loses the battle, he wins Emelye as a wife when Arcite dies.

Emelye

The sister of Hippolyta, she is a pawn within the struggle between Arcite and Palamon, both who have fallen in love with her. Although she wishes to remain chaste in honor of the goddess, Diana, she accepts that she must marry one of the two knights.

Theseus

The King of Athens, he wages war upon Thebes in response to the injustice of the Theban king, and imprisons Arcite and Palamon. He sets the rules and regulations of their duel for Emelye.

Hippolyta

The Queen of Scythia, she is the husband of Theseus, King of Athens, and the sister of Emelye.

Pirithous

A prince and childhood friend of Theseus, he intervenes to have Arcite released from prison on the condition that he never return to Athens.

Lycurgus

The king of Thrace, he fights with Palamon during his duel with Arcite.

Emetreus

The king of India, he fights with Arcite during his duel with Palamon.

John

An oafish carpenter, he is an older man who marries the much younger Alison. He foolishly believes Nicholas' prediction that a second great flood is coming, and hides in a kneading bucket on his roof in preparation for it.

Alison

The crafty wife of John the carpenter, Alison is much younger than her husband. She has an affair with Nicholas, a boarder who stays with her and her husband.

Nicholas

An Oxford student who boards with John and Alison, Nicholas claims to study astronomy. He comes up with the fantastic fabliau "Noah's Ark" trick which makes up most of the plot of the tale.

Absolon

A delicate, courtly lover who pursues Alison, he is a skilled musician and an unabashed romantic. He suffers humiliation at the hands of Alison, but gets revenge on Nicholas.

Symkyn

A vulgar, dishonest and foolish miller, Symkyn repeatedly cheats his customers out of grain. He receives his comeuppance when two Cambridge students that he has cheated seduce his wife and daughter then steal their grain back from him.

Aleyn

A Cambridge student who seduces the miller's daughter, Molly, when he and John stay at the miller's house.

John (2)

A Cambridge student who seduces the miller's wife when he and Aleyn stay at the Miller's house.

Molly

The daughter of the Miller, she is a somewhat unattractive young woman, yet Aleyn nevertheless seduces her when the two students stay at the miller's home.

Constance

The daughter of the Roman emperor, she is given to be married to the Sultan of Syria after he agrees to convert to Christianity. But when his mother opposes this, she narrowly escapes an assassination attempt and ends up in England, where she marries King Alla. After escaping treachery once more, Constance is sent back to Rome. She is a devoted Christian whose faith aids her throughout all of her travails.

The Sultan

The King of Syria, he agrees to convert to Christianity to marry Constance, but his actions infuriate his mother, who has him assassinated.

The Sultana

Villainous mother of the Sultan, she refuses to convert from Islam on the orders of her son and plots his assassination.

Dame Hermengild

The wife of the Warden of the Northumberland region where Constance lands in England, she converts to Christianity through the influence of Constance. A devious knight murders her in an attempt to frame Constance.

The Warden

The husband of Dame Hermengild, he watches over the castle of Northumberland while King Alla is at war. He converts to Christianity along with his wife.

King Alla

The English king of Northumberland, he marries Constance but is separated from her because of the machinations of his mother, Lady Donegild.

Lady Donegild

The treacherous mother of King Alla, she contrives to have Constance and her child banished from England. King Alla murders her for her evil actions.

Mauritius

The son of King Alla and Constance, he becomes the emperor of Rome when Constance's father realizes his royal lineage.

Jankin

The fifth husband of the Wife of Bath, he was much younger than she and prone to reading misogynist religious texts that offended his wife. When he hurt her out of anger, he realized his error and submitted to her authority, after which he and his wife had a perfectly happy marriage.

The Knight (2)

After raping a young woman, the knight is sentenced to death, but spared by the queen, who decides that the knight will receive mercy if he can answer the question "what do women want?"

The Lothly Lady

This elderly woman tells the Knight what women really desire on the condition that he will marry her. When he grants her the authority in marriage, the old woman transforms into a beautiful young woman.

The Summoner (2)

The summoner, who is given no proper name, is a typical representation of his profession, according to the Friar. He meets the devil and shares trade secrets, and is cast into hell for his sinful behavior.

Satan

Introducing himself as a yeoman, he and the summoner become compatriots until he finally casts the summoner into hell.

The Friar

This boorish friar is rude and presumptuous, oblivious to the conditions of Thomas and his wife, who take him in as a boarder. Although ostensibly polite and refined, the friar callously begs Thomas for money.

Thomas

Owner of a home where the Friar stays, his infant child had recently died and he himself has taken ill. When the Friar begs him for money, Thomas pays him with the "gift" of a fart.

Griselde

A woman of low status, she marries Walter, the marquis of Saluzzo, but is subjected to a number of trials that her husband devises to prove her worth. She handles each of these trials honorably, proving herself dedicated and steadfast in the face of any tragedy.

Walter

The marquis of Saluzzo, he is a dedicated bachelor until the people of his region insist that he takes a wife. When he marries Griselde, he subjects her to a number of trials meant to prove her worth, each of them cruel and heartless.

Janicula

The father of Griselde. She returns to him after she has been cast out of her home by Walter.

January

A wealthy knight and perpetual bachelor, at the age of sixty this blind man decides to take a young wife. When he marries May, he bores her with his insistent sexual desire, leading her to have an affair. He regains his sight when Pluto and Proserpina find May having sex with Damian in his presence.

May

The young wife of January, she soon tires of his persistent and monotonous sexual desire and has an affair with January's squire, Damian. When January regains his sight and sees her engaged in a tryst with Damian, she insists that he should not believe his eyes.

Damian

January's squire, he has an affair with May.

Placebo

A friend of January's who argues for the merits of marrying a young woman at such an elderly age.

Pluto

The king of the fairies, he and his wife stumble upon January, May and Damian when the latter two have a sexual encounter. He restores January's sight.

Proserpina

She is the wife of Pluto.

Canacee

The daughter of the King of Tartary, she receives the gift of knowing the language of animals and the healing properties of every herb.

Cambyuskan

The King of Tartary. A mysterious knight brings him a mechanical horse that can transport him anywhere across the globe.

Arviragus

A devoted knight and husband to Dorigen, he travels to Britain to engage in war, causing great grief to his wife. He gives up his wife so that she may preserve her honor.

Dorigen

The wife of Arviragus, she becomes intensely depressed when he leaves for Britain, fearing for his life. She promises to have an affair with Aurelius if he can make the rocks that obstruct the shore on which Arviragus will land disappear.

Aurelius

A young squire who falls in love with Dorigen, he pays the Orleans student to make the rocks off of the Brittany shore disappear so that Dorigen will have an affair with him. But he gives her up when he realizes the pain that it would cause her.

The Orleans Student

A law student skilled in creating apparitions, he contrives to have the rocks off of the Brittany shore disappear, but when Aurelius does not engage in an affair with Dorigen, he forgives Aurelius of his debt for creating the apparition.

Virginius

An honorable and well-loved knight, he murders his daughter when Appius and Claudius scheme to have her raped.

Virginia

The daughter of Virginius, her incomparable beauty leads Appius to lust after her and scheme to have her raped.

Appius

A corrupt judge who governs the town where Virginius resides, he contrives to have Claudius claim that Virginius had stolen his slave from him. When his scheme is revealed, he is taken to jail where he commits suicide.

Claudius

A churl who schemes with Appius, he claims that Virginia is his slave and that Virginius stole her from him. When his treachery is revealed, he is banished.

The Three Rioters

Three indistinguishable troublemakers who engage in all sorts of lewd behavior, they go on a search for Death and end up finding it in the form of gold coins.

The Old Man

An aged man who cannot die, he wishes to trade his body with a younger man. He tells the three rioters where they may find Death.

The Merchant (2)

A devoted entrepreneur, he is somewhat stingy but dedicated to his business and to thrifty behavior. He insists that his wife repay one hundred francs that he lent her, leading her to seek the sum from Dan John.

Dan John

This monk claims to be a cousin of the merchant. He agrees to lend the merchant's life one hundred francs if she has an affair with him, then borrows the sum from the husband that she intends to repay.

The Wife

A dissatisfied wife, she claims that her husband, the merchant, is a stingy man who does not satisfy her. Displeased that her husband wants her to repay a one hundred franc debt, she agrees to an affair with Dan John for that sum. When the merchant offers that he has been repaid in his own money, she tells him that she will repay him through sex.

Melibee

A mighty and rich ruler, his enemies rape his wife and attack his daughter, leading him to strive for a war of retribution - yet his wife implores him to be merciful.

Prudence

The wife of Melibee, she is raped by his enemies, but wishes to grant them mercy.

Sophie

The young daughter of Melibee, she is left for dead by his enemies when they wound her in five places, but nevertheless barely survives.

Chaunticleer

This rooster, peerless in his crowing, has seven companions, the most honored of which is Pertelote. He dreams that he will be chased by a fox, a prophecy that comes true. He is also a strong believer in this prophetic power of dreams. Chaunticleer's name means clear-voiced, or bright-song.

Pertelote

The most favored of Chanticleer's companions, this hen is essentially his 'wife.' She dismisses his idea that dreams predict future events, claiming that his ill temper stems from stomach maladies. But her advice to find healing herbs ultimately leads to the fulfillment of his prophecy.

Cecilia

Devout elite Roman woman who dies for her adherence to Christianity.

Valerian

Eventual husband of Cecilia who converts to Christianity upon the influence of Pope Urban. He is executed for his beliefs.

Pope Urban

Christian leader who baptizes Valerian and Tibertius and claims that Cecilia is a saint.

Tibertius

The brother of Cecilia, he converts to Christianity, but is executed with Valerian for his Christian beliefs.

Almachius

Roman prefect who ordered the deaths of Cecilia, Valerian and Tibertius for their Christian beliefs.

Maximus

Roman sergeant who claimed to see the spirits of Valerian and Tibertius ascending to heaven when they are executed, prompting many to convert to Christianity.

Phoebus

Deity who, when he lived on earth, took a wife who was unfaithful to him, despite his insistence on watching her. He teaches his prized white crow to speak the language of humans.

The Crow

This beautiful white crow can speak the language of humans, having been taught by Phoebus. But when he tells Phoebus that his wife had an affair, Phoebus plucks him and curses him, condemning all crows to be forever black and harsh of voice.

Justinus

A friend of January's who argues against him taking a young wife.

Major Themes

Feminism and anti-feminism

Chaucer was extremely interested in the role of women in society, and how they reacted to it. In the Wife of Bath's Tale, for example, Chaucer foregrounds the issue of female "maistrie", and in the series of Tales often called "the Marriage group" by critics, Chaucer actively explores the potential dynamics of a male-female marriage. In the Middle Ages, feminism had obviously not been invented; but one sees very clearly in the mouth of the Wife of Bath that ideas of female equality were by no means unusual.

Christianity

The Tales as a whole take place on a religious pilgrimage to Canterbury, and Chaucer's "Retraction" makes a famous apology for the way the Tales have a tendency towards sin. Are they blasphemous? Furthermore, is Chaucer's retraction of them genuine? Critics have argued both cases. But what is certain is that the Tales contain a huge amount of religious material, both in the expressly religious tales (the Prioress, the Parson, the Clerk) and in the supposedly non-religious ones (the Summoner, the Miller, the Friar).

Words and language

"What nedeth wordes mo?" ("What more needs to be said?") is a question that is constantly voiced, from the Knight's Tale all the way through the silencing theme of the final tale, the Manciple's. The nature of language, the value of words, whether words can ever have a true "meaning", or whether you can ever really "own" words are all themes which Chaucer scrutinizes at various points during the Tales.

Tellers as dramatic voices

The key structural complication of the Tales is the way that Chaucer situates himself within the fictional pilgrimage, claiming that he is simply recording what other people have said. Thus we are never sure whether any statement is the opinion of the teller (say, the Wife of Bath), of the fictional Chaucer ("Geffrey", as he is referred to in criticism) or of Chaucer himself. It is extremely difficult, due to the dramatic, "ventriloquised" nature of the tale-telling project, to actually ascertain who we are listening to at any one stage.

Fables, fiction and fabliaux

Chaucer is always interested in fables, "moral stories", or genres which have a set pattern - and, to generalise a little, often juxtaposes these fictional, literary traditions with a mode of Middle English realism to see how they co-exist. Thus Chaunticleer in the Nun's Priest's Tale reasons far beyond the means of even the most well-read chicken. Meanwhile, the crow, in the Manciple's Tale, is shunted out of what seems a cartoon-like, fabliau beginning to a tale, to later be physically abused in a shockingly realistic way by the end of it. How does a fictional world relate to the real world? How does a literary tradition match up to the world it represents? Can we ever take a moral from a story?

Quitting, vengeance and paying debts

There are several instances both within tales and across the structure of the work itself where one character resolves to "quit" another. The Miller, for example, quits the Knight's Tale, only to have his tale quit by the Reeve - and later, the Summoner furiously quits the Friar's Tale with his own venemous anti-Friar narrative. Quitting often provides smaller internal structures within the larger structure of the Tales as a whole, and invites the comparison of one thing to another.

Sex and adultery

Many of Chaucer's Tales are interested in the way a marriage might work or fail to work. Look at any of the tales which dramatize adultery or cuckolding (the Miller's, the Reeve's, the Merchant's, the Wife of Bath's, etc.), focusing particularly on the way that sexual activity is depicted. Chaucer's presentation of sex varies wildly, sometimes present only through pointed euphemism (like the Wife's *bele chose*) and sometimes, like in the Reeve's or the Merchant's tales, vividly described.

Justice and judgement

The Franklin's Tale ends with an explicit question to its audience, asking them to consider each of its characters and then decide which they think is the most generous. It is not the only tale to pose questions and invite comparisons of its characters: the Knight's Tale, for example, asks at the end of its first part whether Arcite or Palamon is better off, and the Merchant's Tale opens with a lively debate between Placebo and Justinus about whether January should marry. Chaucer often puts two things together (this could also be interestingly related to the idea of quitting) and invites the evaluation, the judgement, of one versus the other. Note too the moments in Tales when "justice", be it legal (in, say, the Wife of Bath's Tale) or comic (in, say, the Miller's Tale) is ultimately done: it's clear that justice, in Chaucer's world at least, is not always just.

Seriousness and silliness

or "Ernest" and "game", as Chaucer himself calls the duality in the Tales. Many of the comic tales have an undoubtedly serious side or incur serious consequences (the broken arm that John the carpenter suffers during his fall from grace, for example, in the Miller's Tale) and serious tales can often similarly have comic, or ironic moments. The whole tale-telling project remember, is, in the General Prologue, supposed to be "game", but instructive game - namely fun with a moral purpose. Whether the tales fulfill this definition is ultimately up to the reader.

Glossary of Terms

anti-feminist

misogynistic; negative about women

auctorite (or authority)

knowledge gained from texts; written authorities (often classical authors)

auctour (or author)

an author - someone who writes, but particularly someone who writes with "authority" (see below) on a subject

Ave Marie

the Latin for "Hail Mary" - and the title of a Christian song sung by the child in the Prioress' Tale

bele chose

the Wife of Bath's euphemism for her vagina

Boethian

pertaining to the attitudes or writings of Boethius

chapmen

merchants

Chichevache

a legendary cow who eats patient wives

clerk

in medieval English, a scholar - someone learned, who has studied.

coal fox

a fox with black-tipped feet, ears and tail

corage

inclination, sexual desire, determination, courage

cuckold

someone whose wife has been sexually unfaithful to them

ekphrasis

a description in words of something visual: painting with words

experience

life experience, knowledge gained through living: the opposite of "written authority"

fabliau

an old story, presented as poetry in medieval French. Often light-hearted, clever, witty short tales, focused on elaborate tricks, cunning plots or talking animals. The plural of fabliau is fabliaux.

feminism

advocacy of the rights of women, and the equality of the sexes

glossing (or glosynge)

interpreting a text to make it mean something: in medieval times, the textual glosses (explanations) were often written in the margins of texts, and were widely published

hende

a medieval English version of our modern word "handy" - meaning clever, cunning, or practically "good with the hands". Applied, with good reason, to Nicholas in *the Miller's Tale.*

Jankin

a common name for a clerk (and can also be a derogatory name for a priest or friar)

maistrie

the Middle English word for "mastery"

Middle English

The English language in the period between Old English and modern English, usually considered to be from about 1100-50 until about 1450-1500.

O Alma redemptoris

Latin for "Gracious mother of the Redeemer" - the title of a Christian song sung by the child in the Prioress' Tale

occupatio

a description of a situation, while professing to leave it undescribed through lack of knowledge, or unwillingness to discuss it

pardons

A pardon is the forgiveness of a crime. Historically, the Catholic Church used to issue a pardon on paper, which could be bought from a Pardoner for a certain amount of money in order to (quite literally) buy forgiveness and thereby a route to heaven.

Pentecost

the day on which the Holy Spirit was dispersed to Jesus' disciples in the Christian calendar

pilgrimage

a long journey of religious significance. In this case, the pilgrims travel from an inn in Southwark to the shrine of St. Thomas in Canterbury.

Prima pars

First part

proto-feminist

an attitude which shares feminism's values, but which was held or explained before "feminism" (or at least the concept called "feminism") existed

queynte

the middle English version of both our words "quaint" (meaning old-fashioned, coy, pretty) and "cunt" (meaning the female external genitals

quit

a Middle English word which is a close relation of our "requite" - it can either mean to revenge something or repay someone

rime royal

a verse form used by Chaucer in four tales - the Prioress, the Second Nun, the Man of Law, and the Clerk - which have religious themes. It is a seven line stanza, rhymed abab bcc.

Roman de la rose

The "Romance of the Rose" is a French medieval poem which heavily influenced Chaucer. See "Additional Content" section for more detail.

romance

A tale in verse, usually about the adventures of some hero of chivalry, and usually relating to the ideals of courtliness and knighthood

Secunda pars

Second part

sentence

the Middle-English word from which our "sententiousness" derives. Sentence is "meaning", "moral", "meaningfulness", "counsel" - and is a good yardstick by which to judge any of the teller's tales.

summoner

a petty officer who cites and warns persons to appear in court; usually a religious court, and often at the behest of the church

ventriloquism

as used in talking about the Tales, it tends to refer to the way Chaucer adopts another character's voice, without "he said" or "she said", but writing or speaking **as** that character

[to] sette... [someone's] cappe

to make a fool out of someone

Short Summary

The Canterbury Tales begins with the introduction of each of the pilgrims making their journey to Canterbury to the shrine of Thomas a Becket. These pilgrims include a Knight, his son the Squire, the Knight's Yeoman, a Prioress, a Second Nun, a Monk, a Friar, a Merchant, a Clerk, a Man of Law, a Franklin, a Weaver, a Dyer, a Carpenter, a Tapestry-Maker, a Haberdasher, a Cook, a Shipman, a Physician, a Parson, a Miller, a Manciple, a Reeve, a Summoner, a Pardoner, the Wife of Bath, and Chaucer himself. Congregating at the Tabard Inn, the pilgrims decide to tell stories to pass their time on the way to Canterbury. The Host of the Tabard Inn sets the rules for the tales. Each of the pilgrims will tell two stories on the way to Canterbury, and two stories on the return trip. The Host will decide whose tale is best for meaningfulness and for fun. They decide to draw lots to see who will tell the first tale, and the Knight receives the honor.

The Knight's Tale is a tale about two knights, Arcite and Palamon, who are captured in battle and imprisoned in Athens under the order of King Theseus. While imprisoned in a tower, both see Emelye, the sister of Queen Hippolyta, and fall instantly in love with her. Both knights eventually leave prison separately: a friend of Arcite begs Theseus to release him, while Palamon later escapes. Arcite returns to the Athenian court disguised as a servant, and when Palamon escapes he suddenly finds Arcite. They fight over Emelye, but their fight is stopped when Theseus finds them. Theseus sets the rules for a duel between the two knights for Emelye's affection, and each raise an army for a battle a year from that date. Before the battle, Arcite prays to Mars for victory in battle, Emelye prays to Diana that she may marry happily, and Palamon prays to Venus to have Emelye as his wife. All three gods hear their prayers and argue over whose should get precedence, but Saturn decides to mediate. During their battle, Arcite indeed is victorious, but as soon as he is crowned victor, he is killed. Before he dies, he reconciles with Palamon and tells him that he deserves to marry Emelye. Palamon and Emelye marry.

When the Knight finishes his tale, everybody is pleased with its honorable qualities, but the drunken Miller insists that he shall tell the next tale. The Miller's Tale, in many ways a version of the Knight's, is a comic table in which Nicholas, a student who lives with John the carpenter and his much younger wife, Alison, falls in love with Alison. Another man, the courtly romantic Absolon, also falls in love with Alison. Nicholas contrives to sleep with Alison by telling John that a flood equal to Noah's flood will come soon, and the only way that he, Nicholas and Alison will survive is by staying in separate kneading tubs placed on the roof of houses, out of sight of all. While John remained in this kneading tub, Nicholas and Alison leave to have sex, but are interrupted by Absolon, singing to Alison at her bedroom window. She told him to close his eyes and he would receive a kiss. He did so, and she pulled down her pants so that he could kiss her arse. The humiliated Absolon got a hot iron from a blacksmith and returned to Alison. This time, Nicholas tried the same trick, and Absolon branded his backside. Nicholas shouted for water, awakening John, who was asleep on the roof. Thinking the flood had come, he cut the rope and came crashing through the floor of his house, landing in the cellar.

The pilgrims laughed heartily at this tale, but Oswald the Reeve takes offense, thinking that the Miller meant to disparage carpenters. In response, The Reeve's Tale tells the story of a dishonest Miller, Symkyn, who repeatedly cheated his clients, which included a Cambridge college. Two Cambridge students, Aleyn and John, went to the miller to buy meal and corn, but while they were occupied Symkyn let their horses run free and stole their corn. They were forced to stay with Symkyn for the night. That night, Aleyn seduced the miller's daughter, Molly, while John seduced the miller's wife. Thanks to a huge confusion of whose bed is who in the dark, Aleyn tells Symkyn of his exploits, thinking he is John: and the two fight. The miller's wife, awaking and thinking the devil had visited her, hit Symkyn over the head with a staff, knocking him unconscious, and the two students escaped with the corn that Symkyn had stolen.

The Cook's Tale was intended to follow the Reeve's Tale, but this tale only exists as a fragment. Following this tale is the Man of Law's Tale, which tells the story of Constance, the daughter of a Roman emperor who becomes engaged to the Sultan of Syria on the condition that he converts to Christianity. Angered by his order to convert his country from Islam, the mother of the Sultan assassinates her son and Constance barely escapes. She is sent on a ship that lands in Britain, where she is taken in by the warden of a nearby castle and his wife, Dame Hermengild. Both of them soon convert to Christianity upon meeting her. A young knight fell in love with Constance, but when she refused him, he murdered Dame Hermengild and attempted to frame Constance. However, when King Alla made the knight swear on the Bible that Constance murdered Hermengild, his eyes burst. Constance marries King Alla and they have a son, Mauritius, who is born when Alla is at war in Scotland. Lady Donegild contrives to have Constance banished by intercepting the letters between Alla and Constance and replacing them with false ones. Constance is thus sent away again, and on her voyage her ship comes across a Roman ship. A senator returns her to Rome, where nobody realizes that she is the daughter of the emperor. Eventually, King Alla makes a pilgrimage to Rome, where he meets Constance once more, and the Roman emperor realizes that Mauritius is his grandson and names him heir to the throne.

The Wife of Bath begins her tale with a long dissertation on marriage in which she recounts each of her five husbands. Her first three husbands were old men whom she would hector into providing for her, using guilt and refusal of sexual favors. However, the final two husbands were younger men, more difficult to handle. The final husband, Jankin, was a twenty-year-old, half the Wife of Bath's age. He was more trouble, as he refused to let the Wife of Bath dominate him and often read literature that proposed that women be submissive. When she tore a page out of one of his books, Jankin struck her, causing her to be deaf in one ear. However, he felt so guilty at his actions that from that point in the marriage, he was totally submissive to her and the two remained happy. The Wife of Bath's Tale is itself a story of marriage dynamic. It tells the tale of a knight who, as punishment for raping a young woman, is sentenced to death. However, he is spared by the queen, who will grant him freedom if he can answer the question "what do women want?" The knight cannot find a satisfactory answer until he meets an old crone, who promises to tell him the answer if he marries her. He agrees, and receives his freedom when he tells the queen that women want sovereignty over their husbands. However, the knight is dissatisfied that he must marry the old, low-born hag. She therefore tells him that he can have her as a wife either old and ugly yet submissive, or young and beautiful yet dominant. He chooses to have her as a young woman, and although she had authority in marriage the two were completely happy from that point.

The Friar asks to tell the next tale, and asks for pardon from the Summoner, for he will tell a tale that exposes the fraud of that profession. The Friar's Tale tells about a wicked summoner who, while delivering summons for the church court, comes across a traveling yeoman who eventually reveals himself to be the devil himself. The two share trade secrets, and the devil tells him that they will meet again in hell if the summoner continues to pursue his trade. The summoner visits an old woman and issues her a summons, then offers to accept a bribe as a payment to prevent her excommunication. The old woman believes that she is without sin and curses the summoner. The devil then appears and casts the summoner into hell.

The Summoner was enraged by the Friar's Tale. Before he begins his tale, he tells a short anecdote: a friar visited hell and was surprised to see that there were no other friars. The angel who was with him then lifted up Satan's tail and thousands of friars swarmed out from his arse. The Summoner's Tale is an equally vitriolic attack on friars. It tells of a friar who stays with an innkeeper and his wife and bothers them about not contributing enough to the church and not attending recently. When the innkeeper tells him that he was not recently in church because he has been ill and his infant daughter recently died, the friar attempted to placate him and then asked for donations once more. Thomas the innkeeper promised to give the friar a "gift" and gives him a loud fart.

The Clerk, an Oxford student who has remained quiet throughout the journey, tells the next tale on the orders of the Host. The Clerk's Tale recounts a story about Walter, an Italian marquis who finally decides to take a wife after the people of his province object to his longtime status as a bachelor. Walter marries Griselde, a low-born but amazingly virtuous woman whom everybody loves. However, Walter decides to test her devotion. When their first child, a daughter, is born, Walter tells her that his people are unhappy and wish for the child's death. He takes away the child, presumably to be murdered, but instead sends it to his sister to be raised. He does the same with their next child, a son. Finally, Walter tells Griselde that the pope demands that he divorce her. He sends her away from his home. Each of these tragedies Griselde accepts with great patience. Walter soon decides to make amends, and sends for his two children. He tells Griselde that he will marry again, and introduces her to the presumed bride, whom he then reveals is their daughter. The family is reunited once more. The Clerk ends with the advice that women should strive to be as steadfast as Griselde, even if facing such adversity is unlikely and perhaps impossible.

The Merchant praises Griselde for her steadfast character, but claims that his wife is far different from the virtuous woman of the Clerk's story. He instead tells a tale of an unfaithful wife. The Merchant's Tale tells a story of January, an elderly blind knight who decides to marry a young woman, despite the objections of his brother, Placebo. January marries the young and beautiful May, who soon becomes dissatisfied with his sexual attentions to her and decides to have an affair with his squire, Damian, who has secretly wooed her by signs and tokens. When January and May are in their garden, May sneaks away to have sex with Damian. The gods Pluto and Proserpina come upon Damian and May and Pluto restores January's sight so that he may see what his wife is doing. When January sees what is occurring, May tells him not to believe his eyes – they are recovering from the blindness - and he believes her: leading to an on-the-surface happy ending.

The Squire tells the next tale, which is incomplete. The Squire's Tale begins with a mysterious knight arriving at the court of Tartary. This knight gives King Cambyuskan a mechanical horse that can transport him anywhere around the globe and return him within a day. Further, he gives Canacee, the daughter of Cambyuskan, a mirror that can discern honesty and a ring that allows the wearer to know the language of animals and the healing properties of all herbs. Canacee uses this ring to aid a bird who has been rejected in love, but the tale then abruptly ends.

The Franklin's Tale that follows tells of the marriage between the knight Arviragus and his wife, Dorigen. When Arviragus travels on a military expedition, Dorigen laments his absence and fears that, when he returns, his ship will be wrecked upon the rocks off the shore. A young man, Aurelius, falls in love with her, but she refuses to return his favors. She agrees to have an affair with Aurelius only on the condition that he find a way to remove the rocks from the shore, a task she believes impossible. Aurelius pays a scholar who creates the illusion that the rocks have disappeared, while Arviragus returns. Dorigen admits to her husband the promise that she has made, and Arviragus tells her that she must fulfill that promise. He sends her to have an affair with Aurelius, but he realizes the pain that it would cause Dorigen and does not make her fulfill the promise. The student in turn absolves Aurelius of his debt. The tale ends with the question: which of these men behaved most generously and nobly?

The Physician's Tale that follows tells of Virginius, a respected Roman knight whose daughter, Virginia, was an incomparable beauty. Appius, the judge who governed his town, lusted after Virginia and collaborated with Claudius, who claimed in court that Virginia was his slave and Virginius had stolen her. Appius orders that Virginia be handed over to him. Virginius, knowing that Appius and Claudius did this in order to rape his daughter, instead gave her a choice between death or dishonor. She chooses death, and Virginius chops off his daughter's head, which he brings to Appius and Claudius. The people were so shocked by this that they realized that Appius and

Claudius were frauds. Appius was jailed and committed suicide, while Claudius was banished.

The Pardoner prefaces his tale with an elaborate confession about the deceptive nature of his profession. He tells the secrets of his trade, including the presentation of useless items as saints' relics. The Pardoner's Tale concerns three rioters who search for Death to vanquish him. They find an old man who tells them that they may find Death under a nearby tree, but under this tree they only find a large fortune. Two of the rioters send the third into town to purchase food and drink for the night (when they intend to escape with their fortune) and while he is gone they plan to murder him. The third rioter poisons the drink, intending to take all of the money for himself. When he returns, the two rioters stab him, then drink the poisoned wine and die themselves. The three rioters thus find Death in the form of avarice. The Pardoner ends his tale with a diatribe against sin, imploring the travelers to pay him for pardons, and be absolved, but the Host berates him scatalogically into silence.

The next story, The Shipman's Tale, is the story of a thrifty merchant and his wife. The wife tells a monk, the merchant's close friend, that she is unhappy in her marriage, and asks if she might borrow a hundred francs of his. In return for the loan, she agrees, she will sleep with him. The monk then borrows the money from the merchant himself, sleeps with his wife, and pays her her husband's money. When the merchant asks for his money back, the monk tells him it he gave it to the wife: and when the merchant confronts his wife, the wife simply tells him that she will repay the debt to her husband in bed.

The Prioress' Tale tells the story of a young Christian child who lived in a town in Asia that was dominated by a vicious Jewish population. One child learned the "Alma redemptoris", a song praising the Virgin Mary, and traveled home from school singing it. The Jews, angry at his behavior, took the child and slit his throat, leaving him in a cesspit to die. The boy's mother searched frantically for her son. When she found him, he was not yet dead, for the Virgin Mary had placed a grain on his tongue that would allow him to speak until it was removed. When this was removed, the boy passed on to heaven. The story ends with a lament for the young boy and a curse for the Jews who perpetrated the heinous crime.

Chaucer himself tells the next tale, The Tale of Sir Thopas, a florid and fantastical poem in rhyming couplets that serves only to annoy the other pilgrims. The Host interrupts Chaucer shortly into this tale, and tells him to tell another. Chaucer then tells The Tale of Melibee, one of two tales that is in prose (the other is the Parson's Tale). This tale is about Melibee, a powerful ruler whose enemies attack his family. When deciding whether to declare war on his enemies, Prudence, his wife, advises him to remain merciful, and they engage in a long debate over the appropriate course of action. Melibee finally gives his enemies the option: they can receive a sentence either from him or from his wife. They submit to Melibee's judgment, and he intends to disinherit and banish the perpetrators. However, he eventually submits to his wife's plea for mercy.

The Monk's Tale is not a narrative tale at all, but instead an account of various historical and literary figures who experience a fall from grace. These include Adam, Samson, Hercules, King Pedro of Spain, Bernabo Visconti, Nero, Julius Caesar, and Croesus. The Knight interrupts the Monk's Tale, finding his listing of historical tragedies monotonous and depressing, and is backed up by the Host.

The Nun's Priest's Tale tells the story of the rooster Chaunticleer and the hen Pertelote. Chaunticleer was ill one night and had a disturbing dream that he was chased by a fox. He feared this dream was prophetic, but Pertelote assured him that his dream merely stemmed from his imbalanced humours and that he should find herbs to cure himself. Chaunticleer insisted that dreams are signifiers, but finally agreed with his wife. However, Chaunticleer is indeed chased by a fox, and carried off – but is saved when he tricks the fox into opening his mouth, allowing Chaunticleer to fly away.

Chaucer follows this with The Second Nun's Tale. This tale is a biography of Saint Cecilia, who converts her husband and brother to Christianity during the time of the Roman empire, when Christian beliefs were illegal. Her brother and husband are executed for their beliefs, and she herself is cut three times with a sword during her execution, but does not immediately die. Rather, she lingers on for several more days, during which time she orders that her property be distributed to the poor. Upon her death Pope Urban declared her a saint.

After the Second Nun finishes her tale, a Canon (alchemist) and his Yeoman join the band of travelers. The Canon had heard how they were telling tales, and wished to join them. The Yeoman speaks incessantly about the Canon, praising him hugely, but then retracts his praise, annoying the Canon, who suddenly departs. The Yeoman therefore decides to tell a tale about a duplicitous Canon: not, he says, his master. The Canon's Yeoman's Tale is a story of the work of a canon and the means by which they defraud people by making them think that they can duplicate money.

The Host tells the Cook to tell the next tale, but he is too drunk to coherently tell one. The Manciple therefore tells a tale. The Manciple's Tale is the story of how Phoebus, when he assumed mortal form, was a jealous husband. He monitored his wife closely, fearing that she would be unfaithful. Phoebus had a white crow that could speak the language of humans and could sing beautiful. When the white crow learns that Phoebus' wife was unfaithful, Phoebus plucked him of his feathers and threw him out of doors. According to the Manciple, this explains why crows are black and can only sing in an unpleasant tone.

The Parson tells the final tale. The Parson's Tale is not a narrative tale at all, however, but rather an extended sermon on the nature of sin and the three parts necessary for forgiveness: contrition, confession, and satisfaction. The tale gives examples of the seven deadly sins and explains them, and also details what is necessary for redemption. Chaucer ends the tales with a retraction, asking those who were offended by the tales to blame his rough manner and lack of education, for his intentions were not immoral, while asking those who found something redeemable in the tales to give credit to Christ.

Summary and Analysis of General Prologue

"When April comes with his sweet, fragrant showers, which pierce the dry ground of March, and bathe every root of every plant in sweet liquid, then people desire to go on pilgrimages." Thus begins the famous opening to *The Canterbury Tales*. The narrator (a constructed version of Chaucer himself) is first discovered staying at the Tabard Inn in Southwark (in London), when a company of twenty-nine people descend on the inn, preparing to go on a pilgrimage to Canterbury. After talking to them, he agrees to join them on their pilgrimage.

Yet before the narrator goes any further in the tale, he describes the circumstances and the social rank of each pilgrim. He describes each one in turn, starting with the highest status individuals.

The Knight is described first, as befits a 'worthy man' of high status. The Knight has fought in the Crusades in numerous countries, and always been honored for his worthiness and courtesy. Everywhere he went, the narrator tells us, he had a 'sovereyn prys' (which could mean either an 'outstanding reputation', or a price on his head for the fighting he has done). The Knight is dressed in a 'fustian' tunic, made of coarse cloth, which is stained by the rust from his coat of chainmail.

The Knight brings with him his son, **The Squire**, a lover and a lusty bachelor, only twenty years old. The Squire cuts a rather effeminate figure, his clothes embroidered with red and white flowers, and he is constantly singing or playing the flute. He is the only pilgrim (other than, of course, Chaucer himself) who explicitly has literary ambitions: he 'koude songes make and wel endite' (line 95).

The Yeoman (a freeborn servant) also travels along with the Knight's entourage, and is clad in coat and hood of green. The Yeoman is excellent at caring for arrows, and travels armed with a huge amount of weaponry: arrows, a bracer (arm guard), a sword, a buckler, and a dagger as sharp as a spear. He wears an image of St. Christopher on his breast.

Having now introduced the Knight (the highest ranking pilgrim socially), the narrator now moves on to the clergy, beginning with **The Prioress**, called 'Madame Eglantine' (or, in modern parlance, Mrs. Sweetbriar). She could sweetly sing religious services, speaks fluent French and has excellent table manners. She is so charitable and piteous, that she would weep if she saw a mouse caught in a trap, and she has two small dogs with her. She wears a brooch with the inscription 'Amor vincit omnia' ('Love conquers all'). The Prioress brings with her her 'chapeleyne' (secretary), **the Second Nun**.

The Monk is next, an extremely fine and handsome man who loves to hunt, and who follows modern customs rather than old traditions. This is no bookish monk, studying in a cloister, but a man who keeps greyhounds to hunt the hare. The Monk is well-fed, fat, and his eyes are bright, gleaming like a furnace in his head.

The Friar who follows him is also wanton and merry, and he is a 'lymytour' by trade (a friar licensed to beg in certain districts). He is extremely well beloved of franklins (landowners) and worthy woman all over the town. He hears confession and gives absolution, and is an excellent beggar, able to earn himself a farthing wherever he went. His name is Huberd.

The Merchant wears a forked beard, motley clothes and sat high upon his horse. He gives his opinion very solemnly, and does excellent business as a merchant, never being in any debt. But, the narrator ominously remarks, 'I noot how men hym calle' (I don't know how men call him, or think of him).

The Clerk follows the Merchant. A student of Oxford university, he would rather have twenty books by Aristotle than rich clothes or musical instruments, and thus is dressed in a threadbare short coat. He only has a little gold, which he tends to spend on books and learning, and takes huge care and attention of his studies. He never speaks a word more than is needed, and that is short, quick and full of *sentence* (the Middle-English word for 'meaningfulness' is a close relation of 'sententiousness').

The Man of Law (referred to here as 'A Sergeant of the Lawe') is a judicious and dignified man, or, at least, he seems so because of his wise words. He is a judge in the court of assizes, by letter of appointment from the king, and because of his high standing receives many grants. He can draw up a legal document, the narrator tells us, and no-one can find a flaw in his legal writings. Yet, despite all this money and social worth, the Man of Law rides only in a homely, multi-coloured coat.

A Franklin travels with the Man of Law. He has a beard as white as a daisy, and of the sanguine humour (dominated by his blood). The Franklin is a big eater, loving a piece of bread dipped in wine, and is described (though not literally!) as Epicurus' son: the Franklin lives for culinary delight. His house is always full of meat pie, fish and meat, so much so that it 'snewed in his hous of mete and drynke'. He changes his meats and drinks according to what foods are in season.

A Haberdasher and a Carpenter, a Weaver, a Dyer and a Tapycer (weaver of tapestries) are next described, all of them clothed in the same distinctive guildsman's dress. Note that none of these pilgrims, in the end, actually tell a tale.

A Cook had been brought along to boil the chicken up with marrow bones and spices, but this particular Cook knows a draught of ale very well indeed, according to the narrator. The Cook could roast and simmer and boil and fry, make stews and hashes and bake a pie well, but it was a great pity that, on his shin, he has an ulcer.

A Shipman from Dartmouth is next - tanned brown from the hot summer sun, riding upon a carthorse, and wearing a gown of coarse woolen cloth which reaches to his knees. The Shipman had, many times, drawn a secret draught of wine on board ship, while the merchant was asleep. The Shipman has weathered many storms, and knows his trade: he knows the locations of all the harbors from Gotland to Cape Finistere. His shape is called 'the Maudelayne'.

A Doctor of Medicine is the next pilgrim described, clad in red and blue, and no-one in the world can match him in speaking about medicine and surgery. He knows the cause of every illness, what humor engenders them, and how to cure them. He is a perfect practitioner of medicine, and he has apothecaries ready to send him drugs and mixtures. He is well-read in the standard medical authorities, from the Greeks right through to Chaucer's contemporary Gilbertus Anglicus. The Doctor, however, has not studied the Bible.

The Wife of Bath was 'somdel deef' (a little deaf, as her tale will later expand upon) and that was a shame. The Wife of Bath is so adept at making cloth that she surpasses even the cloth-making capitals of Chaucer's world, Ypres and Ghent, and she wears coverchiefs (linen coverings for the head) which must (the narrator assumes) have 'weyeden ten pound'. She had had five husbands through the church door, and had been at Jerusalem, Rome and Boulogne on pilgrimage. She is also described as 'Gat-tothed' (traditionally denoting lasciviousness), and as keeping good company, she knows all the answers about love: 'for she koude of that art the olde daunce' (she knew the whole dance as far as love is concerned!).

A good religious man, **A Parson of a Town**, is next described, who, although poor in goods, is rich in holy thought and work. He's a learned man, who truly preaches Christ's gospel, and devoutly teaches his parishioners. He travels across his big parish to visit all of his parishioners, on his feet, carrying a staff in his hand. He is a noble example to his parishioners ('his sheep', as they are described) because he acts first, and preaches second (or, in Chaucer's phrase, 'first he wroghte, and afterward he taughte'). The narrator believes that there is no better priest to be found anywhere.

With the Parson travels a **Plowman** (who does not tell a tale), who has hauled many cartloads of dung in his time. He is a good, hard-working man, who lives in peace and charity, and treats his neighbor as he would be treated. He rides on a mare, and wears a tabard (a workman's loose garment).

A Miller comes next, in this final group of pilgrims (now at the bottom of the class scale!). He is big-boned and has big muscles, and always wins the prize in wrestling matches. There's not a door that he couldn't lift off its hinges, or break it by running at it head-first. He has black, wide nostrils, carries a sword and a buckler (shield) by his side, and has a mouth like a great furnace. He's good at stealing corn and taking payment for it three times. But then, Chaucer implies, there are no honest millers.

A noble Manciple (a business agent, purchaser of religious provisions) is the next pilgrim to be described, and a savvy financial operator. Though a common man, the Manciple can run rings round even a 'heep of lerned men'. The Manciple, his description ominously ends, 'sette hir aller cappe': deceived them all.

The **Reeve**, a slender, choleric man, long-legged and lean ("ylyk a staf"). He knows exactly how much grain he has, and is excellent at keeping his granary and his grain bin. There is no bailiff, herdsman or servant about whom the Reeve does not know something secret or treacherous; as a result, they are afraid of him 'as of the deeth'.

The Summoner is next, his face fire-red and pimpled, with narrow eyes. He has a skin disease across his black brows, and his beard (which has hair falling out of it) and he is extremely lecherous. There is, the narrator tells us, no ointment or cure, or help him to remove his pimples. He loves drinking wine which is as 'reed as blood', and eating leeks, onions and garlic. He knows how to trick someone.

Travelling with the Summoner is a noble **Pardoner**, his friend and his companion (in what sense Chaucer intends the word 'compeer', meaning companion, nobody knows) and the last pilgrim-teller to be described. He sings loudly 'Come hither, love to me', and has hair as yellow as wax, which hangs like flaxen from his head. He carries a wallet full of pardons in his lap, brimful of pardons come from Rome. The Pardoner is sexually ambiguous - he has a thin, boyish voice, and the narrator wonders whether he is a 'geldyng or a mare' (a eunuch or a homosexual).

The narrator writes that he has told us now of the estate (the class), the array (the clothing), and the number of pilgrims assembled in this company. He then makes an important statement of intent for what is to come: he who repeats a tale told by another man, the narrator says, must repeat it as closely as he possibly can to the original teller - and thus, if the tellers use obscene language, it is not our narrator's fault.

The **Host** is the last member of the company described, a large man with bright, large eyes - and an extremely fair man. The Host welcomes everyone to the inn, and announces the pilgrimage to Canterbury, and decides that, on the way there, the company shall 'talen and pleye' (to tell stories and amuse themselves). Everyone consents to the Host's plan for the game, and he then goes on to set it out.

What the Host describes is a tale-telling game, in which each pilgrim shall tell two tales on the way to Canterbury, and two more on the way home; whoever tells the tale 'of best sentence and moost solas' shall have supper at the cost of all of the other pilgrims, back at the Inn, once the pilgrimage returns from Canterbury. The pilgrims agree to the Host's suggestion, and agree to accord to the Host's judgment as master of the tale-telling game. Everyone then goes to bed.

The next morning, the Host awakes, raises everyone up, and 'in a flok' the pilgrimage rides towards 'the Wateryng of Seint Thomas', a brook about two miles from London. The Host asks the pilgrims to draw lots to see who shall tell the first tale, the Knight being asked to 'draw cut' first and, whether by 'aventure, or sort, or cas', the Knight draws the straw to tell the first tale. The pilgrims ride forward, and the

Knight begins to tell his tale.

Analysis

The General Prologue was probably written early in the composition of the Canterbury Tales, and offers an interesting comparison point to many of the individual tales itself. Of course, it does not match up to the tales as we have them in a number of ways: the Nun's Priest and the Second Nun are not described, and, most significantly, the work as we have it does not reflect the Host's plan. For starters, the pilgrimage only seems to go as far as Canterbury (for the *Parson's Tale*) and only the narrator tells two tales on the way there, with all the other pilgrims telling only a single tale (and some who are described in the General Prologue not telling a tale at all).

We must, therefore, view the General Prologue with some hesitation as a comparison point to the tales themselves: it offers useful or enlightening suggestions, but they are no means a complete, reliable guide to the tales and what they mean. What the General Prologue offers is a brief, often very visual description of each pilgrim, focusing on details of their background, as well as key details of their clothing, their food likes and dislikes, and their physical features. These descriptions fall within a common medieval tradition of portraits in words (which can be considered under the technical term *ekphrasis*), Chaucer's influence in this case most likely coming from *The Romaunt de la Rose*.

Immediately, our narrator insists that his pilgrims are to be described by 'degree'. By the fact that the Knight, the highest-ranking of the pilgrims, is selected as the first teller, we see the obvious social considerations of the tale. Still, all human life is here: characters of both sexes, and from walks of life from lordly knight, or godly parson down to oft-divorced wife or grimy cook.

Each pilgrim portrait within the prologue might be considered as an archetypal description. Many of the 'types' of characters featured would have been familiar stock characters to a medieval audience: the hypocritical friar, the rotund, food-loving monk, the rapacious miller are all familiar types from medieval estates satire (see Jill Mann's excellent book for more information). Larry D. Benson has pointed out the way in which the characters are paragons of their respective crafts or types - noting the number of times the words 'wel koude' and 'verray parfit' occur in describing characters.

Yet what is key about the information provided in the General Prologue about these characters, many of whom *do* appear to be archetypes, is that it is among the few pieces of objective information - that is, information spoken by our narrator that we are given throughout the Tales. The tales themselves (except for large passages of the prologues and epilogues) are largely told in the words of the tellers: as our narrator himself insists in the passage. The words stand for themselves: and we interpret them as if they come from the pilgrims' mouths. What this does - and this is a key thought for interpreting the tales as a whole - is to apparently strip them of writerly license, blurring the line between Chaucer and his characters.

Thus all of the information might be seen to operate on various levels. When, for example, we find out that the Prioress has excellent table manners, never allowing a morsel to fall on her breast, how are we to read it? Is this Geoffrey Chaucer 'the author of *The Canterbury Tales*' making a conscious literary comparison to *The Romaunt de la Rose*, which features a similar character description (as it happens, of a courtesan)? Is this 'Chaucer' our narrator, a character within the Tales providing observation entirely without subtext or writerly intention? Or are these observations - supposedly innocent within the Prologue - to be noted down so as to be compared later to the Prioress' Tale?

Chaucer's voice, in re-telling the tales as accurately as he can, entirely disappears into that of his characters, and thus the Tales operates almost like a drama. Where do Chaucer's writerly and narratorial voices end, and his characters' voices begin? This self-vanishing quality is key to the Tales, and perhaps explains why there is one pilgrim who is not described at all so far, but who is certainly on the pilgrimage - and he is the most fascinating, and the most important by far: a poet and statesman by the name of Geoffrey Chaucer.

Summary and Analysis of The Knight's Tale

The Knight's Tale

(I)

The Knight begins his tale with the story of Theseus, a prince, who married Hippolyta, the queen of Scythia, and brought her and her sister, Emelye, back to Athens with him after conquering her kingdom of Amazons. When Theseus returned home victorious, he became aware of a company of women clad in black who knelt at the side of the highway, shrieking. The oldest of the women asked Theseus for pity. She told him that she was once the wife of King Cappaneus who was destroyed at Thebes, and that all of the other women lost their husbands. Creon, the lord of the town, had simply tossed the dead bodies of the soldiers in a single pile and refused to burn or bury them.

Theseus swore vengeance upon Creon, and immediately ordered his armies toward Thebes. Theseus vanquished Creon, and when the soldiers were disposing of the bodies they found two young knights, Arcite and Palamon, two royal cousins, not quite dead. Theseus ordered that they be imprisoned in Athens for life. They passed their time imprisoned in a tower in Athens until they saw Emelye in a nearby garden. Both fell immediately in love with her. Palamon compared her to Venus, and prayed escape from the prison; similarly, Arcite claimed that he would rather be dead than not have Emelye. The two fight over her, each calling the other a traitor.

This happened on a day in which Pirithous, a prince and childhood friend of Theseus, had come to Athens. Pirithous had known Arcite at Thebes, and at his request, Theseus set Arcite free on the promise that Arcite would never again be seen in Theseus' kingdom. He now had his freedom, but not the ability to pursue Emelye, and lamented the cruelty of fate. Palamon, however, envied Arcite, since he did now have the option of raising an army against Theseus to conquer Athens. The Knight asks which of the nobles has it worse: Arcite, who has his freedom but not access to Emelye, or Palamon, who can see Emelye but remains a prisoner?

(II)

Two years passed. After spending two years in Thebes, one night Arcite dreamt that he saw the god Mercury standing before him, bidding him to be free of hope and care, and telling him to go to Athens to relieve his grief. Arcite decided to disguise himself, return to Athens and pass unknown.

Arriving at the court, Arcite offered his services, and took a post with Emelye's steward under the name of Philostratus. Arcite worked as a page in Emelye's house and was so well loved that Theseus soon made him squire of his chamber.

Meanwhile Palamon had lived for seven years in his dungeon, before, eventually, he escaped from the tower and fled the city, with the intention of disguising himself and making toward Thebes. That morning Arcite went horseback riding. In the area outside of the city, he dismounted and began to speak to himself, lamenting life without Emelye. Palamon, overhearing, leapt out and revealed himself to Arcite. Since neither had weapons, they made a vow to meet in the same place tomorrow and fight to the death over Emelye.

They returned the next day armed for battle. At the same time, and in the same place, Theseus, Hippolyta and Emelye were out hunting, and, reaching the area where Arcite and Palamon were fighting, Theseus stopped the battle. Palamon told Theseus that Arcite is the man who was banished (and that he has returned, disguised as Philostratus), while he himself is the escaped prisoner. He also told Theseus that both men love Emelye. Theseus ordered the death of both, but the queen and Emelye took pity on the two men, and begged Theseus for mercy. Considering how much they loved Emelye to risk death by not escaping to Thebes, Theseus asked them to swear that they will never make war against any realm of his. Theseus then decided that the two will wage war on each other, each with one hundred knights, in order to decide whom Emelye will marry.

(III)

Theseus commissioned the building of a stadium a mile in circumference for the duel between Arcite and Palamon. This stadium was opulent, featuring carvings and portraits as well as temples honoring Mars, Diana and Venus. When the day of the duel approached, Palamon brought Lycurgus, the king of Thrace, to fight with him, while Arcite brought Emetreus, the king of India.

The night before the duel, Palamon prayed to Venus to solace his pains of love, asking Venus (goddess of love) to let Arcite murder him if Arcite will be the one to marry Emelye. The statue of Venus shook, an omen that the goddess was listening. Emelye prayed at the shrine to Diana, the goddess of chastity. She prayed that she could remain a maiden all her life and not be a man's lover nor wife. She prayed, moreover, for peace and friendship between Arcite and Palamon. But if it was to be her destiny to marry one against her will, she asked to have the one who wants her most. The statue of Diana shed tears of blood, another omen. Then Diana herself appeared to Emelye and told her that she will marry one of the two. Arcite prayed to Mars. He prayed for victory in battle, and the statue of Mars whispered the word "victory" to him, the third omen. Mars and Venus thus waged war upon one another, but aged Saturn found a means to satisfy both of them. He told Venus that Palamon would have his lady, but Mars would help his servant.

(IV)

Theseus set the rules of the battle between the two opposing factions. He ordered that, during the war between the two sides, nobody would suffer a mortal blow. If an opponent was overcome, he was to leave the battle. The people raised their voices in exultation. The two armies were equal in prowess, age and nobility, and Arcite pursued Palamon viciously, and Palamon returned with equal severity. But Emetreus seized Palamon and pierced him with his sword. In the attempt to rescue Palamon, King Lycurgus was struck down, and then Emetreus himself was wounded. Theseus declared that Arcite had won. Venus was disappointed at the outcome, but Saturn told her that Mars was now appeased and she would receive a similar appeasement. Suddenly, as Arcite was proclaimed victorious, there was an earthquake sent by Pluto that frightened Arcite's horse, which swerved and fell, throwing off Arcite and mortally wounding him. Before he died, Arcite tells Emelye that she could have no more worthy husband than Palamon. His last word before he died was her name. Theseus, in a very long speech referred to as the "First Mover" speech, then ordered Emelye to marry Palamon after a funeral ceremony honoring Arcite: and the Knight's story finishes on a happy note.

Analysis

It is very likely that the Knight's Tale was written before the Canterbury Tales as a whole project was planned, and so it has the unusual status of being both a part of the tales as a whole, but also a separate work of literature in its own right (though the text has been adapted into the Tales – lines 875-92). It is a very free adaptation of a story by an Italian writer, Boccaccio, whom it seems clear Chaucer very much admired. Chaucer – as he regularly does – hugely compresses the story into the Tale, and adds material heavily influenced by his philosophical hero Boethius (including Theseus' "First Mover" speech).

The Tale is undoubtedly a *romance* as Chaucer presents it, supposedly a true history of many hundreds of years ago told by an authoritative, high-status figure (in this case the Knight). Yet Chaucer never merely adopts a literary tradition without commenting on it, and the oddities of the Tale often lie in the way it over-stresses the traditional things expected of a romance of its genre.

For example, the question of status (raised at the end of the General Prologue when the Host – perhaps duplicitously – has the Knight picked as the first teller) and rank is immediately raised by the progression of the tale. The Knight begins not with the main characters of the tale, Arcite and Palamon, but instead, he begins at the apex of society, describing the exploits of Theseus of Athens, working downward until he reaches the less distinguished Theban soldiers.

Moreover, the tale is deeply improbable in all sorts of ways, and the situation and the moral questions it poses seem more important than the qualities of the individual characters. Characters, in fact, exist only to be moved by the events of the story: to be imprisoned and set free whenever the plot demands, or to fall in love at first sight when it is dramatically convenient. Even the characters acknowledge their lack of free will within the story. The two knights pray to Venus for a literal *deus ex machine*, for they are unable to control their own fate. The Knight's Tale very openly acknowledges the role of fate through the gods: Palamon leaves his fate to theology, blaming his fate on Venus, Juno and Saturn.

Arcite and Palamon as characters, then, without any real autonomy and speaking only formal, elegant laments, are virtually indistinguishable from each another. There is no information on which a reader may base an opinion on their respective virtues. Emelye is equally something of a cardboard-cutout, rather than a fully rounded character (compare her, for example, with the garrulous, fully-individualised Wife of Bath). The Knight describes her as a typical fairy-tale maiden – though there is an interesting inversion of the usual formula in that her suitors, not her, are the ones imprisoned in a tower. She even first appears in a garden, a pastoral symbol that balances both purity and fertility.

Emelye proves a problematic character in the scheme of the story. Arcite and Palamon are prepared to fight to the death for her love, despite the fact that neither have had any significant contact with her, nor have any idea whether she would love either man. Yet Theseus accepts this code of conduct and offers the queen's sister as a prize for the two men, whom he previously had imprisoned and had threatened with death only moments before.

The Knight's Tale adheres to traditional values of chivalric, knightly honor in which there are strict codes of behavior which one must follow. This code of chivalry is not necessarily polite and decent, and Chaucer is always keen to draw attention to how unheroic such behavior seems. Within the morality of the tale, for example, Theseus' sudden decision to ransack Thebes to right a wrong is perfectly acceptable as punishment for a transgression against the honor of the dead soldiers; modern and medieval readers alike might feel somewhat differently. Finding them fighting, Theseus condemns condemns Arcite's and Palamon's actions not because they were fighting, but because they did not do so under the proper rules of a duel.

One interpretation of the tale might therefore see Chaucer as almost parodying – showing the ridiculousness of – such masculine, chivalric codes. Or is Chaucer rather parodying the genre – romance – in which such actions are endorsed? Immediately, in this first tale, the looming question of tone hangs over the tale. Where does the Knight's voice stop and Chaucer's begin? If there is parody involved in this tale, is it supposed to sit in Chaucer's mouth, or in the Knight's? The dramatic nature of the tales themselves make it extremely difficult to pin them down to a single, univocal interpretation.

Emelye is also the first of a series of interesting portrayals of females in the Tales. Emelye is, almost, a stereotype of a female character: though, significantly, her will is laid out as entirely separate to her actions. She does not wish to marry either of the knights, preferring a life of chastity to marriage. However, she acknowledges her role as a pawn in the situation, and accepts the destiny proscribed to her by the goddess Diana and the mortal king Theseus (even at the end, married off by Theseus, she receives the husband she explicitly does not desire).

The Knight, like the genre of the romance itself, has a tendency toward lush description, elaborate phrasing, and within his tale, things keep becoming displays of wealth and power. Each of the final events in the story is punctuated by great pageantry. Take, for example, the transformation of the simple duel between Arcite and Palamon into a gala event requiring the construction of a massive coliseum for two armies to wage war on one another, even bringing in the kings of two foreign nations. Other books tell the Knight's story "more playn" (1464), according to the tale, and we can quite believe it. Yet it is precisely the dressed-up chivalry of the Knight's tale that makes it very difficult to discern precisely what answer it is proposing to its key question: "What is this world? What asketh men to have?" (2777).

Summary and Analysis of The Miller's Tale

The Miller's Prologue

After the Knight finishes telling his story, it meets with the approval of the whole company. The Host then moves to the Monk (another high-status teller) to tell "somewhat to quite with the Knyghtes tale". It is at this point that the Miller, extremely drunk, interrupts "in Pilates voys", proclaiming that he has a tale that will quit the Knight's.

The Host tries to dissuade the Miller, telling him "thou art a fool", and that he is drunk – a statement with which the Miller immediately agrees. The Miller starts to introduce a tale about how a clerk "set the cappe of" (made a fool out of) a carpenter and his wife, but is immediately interrupted by the Reeve (himself a carpenter) who tries to silence him. The Miller, though, refuses to be dissuaded by the Reeve's argument that tales should not be told about adulterous wives, claiming that

> An housbonde shal nat been inquisityf

Of Goddes pryvetee, nor of his wyf.

Yet before the Miller's Tale itself begins, our narrator makes another interruption to the story's flow, repeating a sentiment he already voiced in the General Prologue: that the tale he is about to repeat is not his own, but the Miller's. Our narrator has no evil intent in rehearsing such a tale, but he must repeat all the tales told – otherwise, he will be falsifying his material.Thus, should any readers find it offensive, they should turn over the leaf and choose another tale. Men, the prologue finishes, should not "maken ernest of game"; find a serious moral in trivial things.

The Miller's Tale

A rich carpenter lived at Oxford, with his wife and a clerk, an impoverished student of astrology and constellations: this clerk was called "hende" (crafty, or cunning) Nicholas. The carpenter had recently wedded a wife, only eighteen years old, who he protected fiercely – because, as she was young and he old, he knew he might well be cuckolded.

One day, while the carpenter was at Osney, Nicholas fell to playing and teasing with this young wife, Alison, and caught her "by the queynte", telling her that he'd die for love of her and holding her hard by the hip-bones. She sprang away from him, refusing to kiss him, but he followed her, crying mercy and speaking fairly: and eventually, she agreed to sleep with him. However, the wife worried, as her husband was so jealous and protective, it would be difficult to find an opportunity – Nicholas resolved to beguile his master, and the two agreed to wait for an opportunity.

Another clerk in the parish, Absolon, who had curly, golden hair, was also mad with desire for Alison, and used to sing at her window at night-time, wooing her until he was woebegone. But, of course, there was no point in Absolon's wooing: Alison was so in love with Nicholas, that Absolon might as well go and whistle.

Meanwhile, Nicholas had come up with a plan. Nicholas told Alison to tell John (the carpenter) that he was ill, and lay in his chamber all weekend, until – on Sunday night – the carpenter sent his slave to knock on the door on check that Nicholas was in health. The slave looked through the keyhole, and seeing Nicholas' eyes gaping upward as if possessed, called to the carpenter, who – seeing Nicholas – panicked, and attributed Nicholas' state to his interest in astrology. Nicholas, he thought, had seen the secrets of God, and gone mad. Having ordered his slave to knock down Nicholas' door, the carpenter awoke Nicholas from his "trance" and the two began to speak.

Nicholas (all going exactly to his plan) swore John to secrecy, and promised to tell him of Christ's counsel. John was aghast as Nicholas told him that, according to his reading of the moon, next Monday, a flood akin to Noah's flood would drown the world in less than an hour. With the carpenter terrified, Nicholas proceeded to the next stage of his plan: that, in the manner of Noah, John was to take large wooden troughs, one for each for Nicholas, Alison and John, and hang them up in the roof (full of supplies) so that no-one can see them, sit in them, and wait. Then, when the water arrives, all John would have to do is take an axe, cut the cord, break a hole in the gable, and float away with his wife and his clerk intact.

Moreover, Nicholas continued, God had requested that, lying in their troughs on the Monday in question, nobody spoke a word - and the carpenter's and his wife's troughs should be hung far apart. The credulous carpenter instantly assented, and went off to make preparations, finding troughs and stocking up food.

Monday arrived, and, as night drew in, the three climbed up to the roof. In their troughs, the three of them prayed, and then the carpenter (probably worn out from all his business setting up the troughs) fell fast asleep, snoring. Nicholas and Alison sped down the ladder, and "withouten words mo they goon to bedde", where they remain until the "laudes" bell (a bell for a church service before daybreak) rang.

Absolon, meanwhile had got some information about John the carpenter, and, thinking that John was away from his house, went to sing to Alison and woo her at a low, hinged window which only came up to his breast height. After a first, gentle song, Alison appeared at the window and gave him short shrift - telling him that she loved somebody else, and warning him that she would "caste a ston" unless he went away. Absolon promised to go away if she would kiss him, once.

Alison tells Nicholas to be quiet and watch her: she then unlocks the window, and, as Absolon leans in to give her a kiss, she puts her naked ass out of the window, which Absolon kisses "ful savourly", feeling, as he does it, something rough and long-haired. "Tehee!" says Alison, and slams the window, and Nicholas and her openly mock Absolon from behind the window. Absolon hears it, and resolves to "quyte" the lovers.

Absolon, moving away from the window, continually says "allas!", sometimes weeping like a beaten child. By the time he arrived at a blacksmith called don Gerveys, Absolon didn't care a bean for Alison, and persuaded his friend to lend him the hot poker in the chimney. Holding it by the cold steel, Absolon returns to the carpenter's window, and knocks again, promising Alison that he has brought her a ring which his mother gave him.

Nicholas had got up "to pisse", and thought he would make the joke even funnier – pulling up the window, he put his ass out of the window for Absolon to kiss. Absolon then asked Alison to speak, so he can see where she is, and Nicholas, at this moment, lets fly a fart "as greet as it had been a thunder-dent", so loud that it almost blinds Absolon. But Absolon was ready with his hot iron, and seized his chance, branding Nicholas' arse.

Nicholas, almost dying of his burning pain, cried out for "Water!", and that cry, awoke John the carpenter from his slumber; thinking Nicholas referred to the flood "Water!", John, sitting up "withouten wordes mo", cut the cord with the axe, bringing everything crashing down from the roof, through the floors, until finally landed on the cellar floor, knocked out.

Nicholas and Alison ran out into the street, crying for attention, and the neighbors ran into look at John, who still lay swooning on the floor, pale and white, his arm broken by the huge fall. And, when he opened his mouth to explain himself, he was shouted down by Nicholas and Alison, who claimed he was mad, being frightened of something as ridiculous as Noah's flood. People laughed at his fantasy, staring into the roof of his smashed house, and turning all of his hurt into a joke – and everything that John argued to preserve his dignity was ignored. Thus ends the Miller's Tale.

Analysis

"Game" and "ernest" are two important concepts in reading the Tales representing respectively jokiness, frivolousness and fun, and seriousness, morality and meaningfulness. Yet one of the things the Miller's Tale makes clear is that it becomes very difficult to decide what is lighthearted fun and what is meaningful, moral telling. The story of John the carpenter is grounded in reality: the details of the story all make sense, and it appears to be set within a suburban, believable Oxford that Chaucer might have known. Yet the story itself is clearly a fabliau: and its sources confirm its debt to fabliau - a hugely elaborate trick, set up with huge care in the story, which snaps shut as the story ends. Immediately "realism" is juxtaposed with "fantasy".

The same problem is bequeathed directly to the reader at the end of the tale: when, after the glorious moment at which John comes crashing down through the roof, and our pleasure in Nicholas' elaborate trick stops, Chaucer suddenly focuses on John's pain. The result of the elaborate trick is an old man, lying unconscious, pale and wan, with a broken arm on his cellar floor - his house destroyed, his wife cuckolded. Is Chaucer doing precisely what the narrator tells us, at the end of the prologue, we musn't do, and making "ernest" of "game"? Maybe – and the Tales as a whole tread a careful, ambiguous line between the serious and the comic.

The same ambiguity of tone is applied to the Christian theme which runs throughout the tale. John the carpenter's plan involves floating up through the roof in his kneading tub when the flood comes; and yet the tale replaces his idealistic upward movement with a crashing downward movement, through his house to the cellar floor. Christian uplift is replaced with a rather damning fall. We might usefully compare this to the fall in discourse and in subject matter from the Knight's Tale to the Miller's Tale: a step downward for the tales themselves as a linear movement (as the Host seems to know full well) in Middle English class distinction – a noble knight to a churlish, drunken miller. Metaphorically speaking, John the carpenter isn't the only thing to come crashing down in this tale.

Is this, then, a blasphemous version of Christianity? Well, it all depends how seriously we read it. If we are offended by Absolon's devilish transformation at the end of the tale (into a blackened devil carrying a flaming iron), or if we recognise the alignment of Alison and Nicholas with Adam and Eve (and the respective falls from grace which follow), then perhaps we might view the tale as deliberately depicting sin. And yet, even though the tale itself is a comic delight - and there is a tremendous amount of pleasure to be had from reading it - the Miller's Tale is far from a negative, anti-type example of sinners in action.

It's also instructive to note the pleasure of the trick in the Miller's Tale, and the fabliau trick rules it demonstrates. The plot within the tale is hugely clever and elaborate, studded with religious imagery: indeed, when John the Carpenter is mentioned as regularly leaving the house, you wonder why the two didn't just sleep together when he was out? The answer can only be because of the sheer pleasure in executing such a complex structure. The tale moves extremely quickly from plot point to plot point, and everyone (except - and this is significant - Alison) is outsmarted. Even ingenious Nicholas ends up wounded on the buttock. In fabliau, you are only as good as your last trick.

Language is also undergoing a fall from grace in the Miller's Tale. Summarize the tale and note how little of its action depends on words or dialogue: unlike the long, protracted speeches of the Knight's Tale, the drunken Miller deals in bodily noises. The mechanics of the tale itself twist on a series of non-verbal sounds, bodily noises and one-word exclamations: Absolon's twice knocking at the window, Alison's cry of "Tehee!" as she closes the window the first time, and Nicholas' final, cumulative cry of "Water!". "Withouten wordes mo" is a key phrase in the Canterbury Tales -

marking moments at which action is more important than words. The courtly language of the Knight becomes furtive, silent stealing to bed without words in the Miller's Tale.

The degradation – or the problematization – of the whole question of language is present throughout the tales, and draws our attention to the warning the narrator gives us before the Tale itself, that he is only "rehearsing" or repeating the words of the Miller. The narrator retells us the words of the Miller, who, telling his tale, repeats the "Tehee!" and "Water!" of Alison and Nicholas. What use – what poetry – what value have these second or third hand words? What do they signify? And most importantly, how far should we read them as belonging to the Miller, to the narrator, or to Chaucer himself?

Summary and Analysis of The Reeve's Tale

The Reeve's Prologue

The company laughs at the foolish story of Nicholas and Absolon. But the narrator notes that Oswald the Reeve alone is angry because he was a carpenter, like John, the butt of the joke in the Miller's Tale. The Reeve then speaks, claiming that, despite his age, he still cunning, and that the qualities of boasting, lying, anger and greed pertain particularly to the elderly. The Host interrupts this rather bitter monologue, pushing the Reeve to tell his tale if he is to speak at all. The Reeve then promises to "answere" and to some extent "sette [the Miller's] howve" ("set his hood" – make a fool out of him). The Miller has scornfully told a tale, the Reeve continues, about how a carpenter was tricked. The Reeve resolves to "quit" the Miller's Tale.

The Reeve's Tale

At Trumpington, near Cambridge, there was a brook upon which stood a mill. The miller who lived there wore ostentatious clothing and could play the bagpipes, wrestle and fish. He also was heavily armed: carrying a "panade" (a cutlass) in his belt, a "joly popper" (small dagger) in his pouch, and a "Sheffeld thwitel" (a Sheffield knife) in his trousers. Bald as an ape, with a round face and flattened nose, this miller's name was Symkyn, and he was a dishonest thief, cheating money out of King's Hall, a Cambridge college, and stealing meal and corn.

His wife came from a noble family, and she was as haughty as ditch-water - "stinking with pride" as the OED has it. The couple had a twenty year-old daughter, and a son who was only six months old and lay in his cradle. The daughter was a large girl with a pug nose, broad buttocks and high, round breasts (though, the narrator is at pains to point out, she did have nice hair).

Two Cambridge students, John and Aleyn, received permission from the master of the college to see the corn ground at the mill - and resolved not to let the dishonest miller cheat them out of even half a grain of corn. The two clerks arrived at the mill, and greeted Symkyn, telling him they were there to grind their corn and take it back to the college. While they ground the corn in the mill, Symkyn crept outside, found the clerks' horse, and set it loose.

Their cornmeal ground and bagged into sacks, the clerks stepped outside to discover that their horse had run away; Aleyn, almost out of his mind with frustration, forgot all about the corn. The miller's wife claimed that the horse had run off to the fen with some wild horses, and the two gullible clerks ran off toward the fen. With them out of the picture, the miller took half a bushel of their flour, and told his wife to go and make a loaf of bread out of it, satisfied with himself for outwitting the clerks. Meanwhile, the two clerks ran up and down, spending hours chasing their horse, until, at almost night-time, they caught him in a ditch.

Returning, weary and wet, the two arrived at the mill, finding the miller sitting by the fire, and they begged for his help. Though my house is narrow, the miller joked, I'm sure you'll be able to make it seem bigger: because clerks can "by arguments make a place / A myle brood of twenty foot of space" (4123-4). Symkyn let the two clerks stay the night, providing ale and bread and a roast goose for dinner.

Symkyn then made them a bed up in his own room, only ten or twelve feet from his own bed. His daughter also had a bed in the same chamber. At midnight, the party had finished eating, and went to bed, the miller's head shining with the alcohol he had drunk. The miller and his wife got into bed, placing the baby's cradle at the foot of their bed, and the clerks and the daughter followed suit. Shortly, the miller began to snore. Before much longer, his wife and daughter were joining in, and the noise was such that you could have heard it two furlongs hence.

Aleyn, kept awake by the snoring, prodded John (next to him in the bed), and resolved to have sex with the miller's daughter, in revenge for the corn that he felt sure the miller had stolen from them. John warned him not to wake the miller – but Aleyn didn't care for his advice, and proceeded straight to the daughter's bed, where he very quickly achieved his aim: and continued to achieve it all night.

John, alone in his bed, felt jealous of Aleyn (still having sex with the miller's daughter) and decided to get some of the action for himself - taking the baby's cradle from the foot of the miller's bed and placing it at the foot of his own. Shortly after this, the miller's wife woke up to go "for a pisse" (4215), and, coming back into the bedroom, felt around in the dark for the cradle – of course, it wasn't at the foot of her bed, but at the foot of John's. As she climbed into the bed, John jumped on her, and gave her, "so myrie a fit ne hadde she nat ful yore" ("the sort of good time she hadn't had for ages"). The two clerks thus lay happily occupied until the third cock crew.

Leaving the bed as the morning dawned, Aleyn was told by the miller's daughter the location of the loaf of bread made from the corn the miller had stolen. Aleyn crept back to the bed, feeling for the cradle, and finding it with his hand. Thinking that the cradle signified the miller's bed, Aleyn thought he had the wrong bed, and so continued on toward the next bed, and, finding no cradle at its foot, crept in beside the miller. Taking him by the neck, he spoke to him softly - telling "John" to wake up and make ready to leave, as he had been copulating with the miller's daughter all night.

"Ye, false harlot, hast?" said the miller, catching Alayn by his Adam's apple and punching him in the face, causing blood to run down Aleyn's chest. The two men rolled, fighting, on the floor like two pigs in a poke, up one minute and down the next, until the miller tripped on a stone and fell backwards onto his sleeping wife.

The miller's wife, thinking a devil had visited her, began to cry out in panic to God, and to her husband to wake up and help her, as she thought the two clerks were fighting. With that, John awoke, and tried to find a stick to help her – but the wife, who knew the room better than John, found it first. Seeing a "litel shymeryng of a light" reflecting the moon's light, and thinking it Aleyn's nightcap, the miller's wife brought down the staff hard onto the miller's bald skull. "Harrow! I dye" he cried, and fell down. The clerks gave him a beating, dressed themselves, took their horse, their corn and their loaf of bread, and escaped.

The Reeve makes a final proverb at the end of his tale, "One who does evil should not expect good", before concluding with God's blessing on the company, adding finally that he has now "quyt the Millere in my tale".

Analysis

From the beginning of its prologue, The Reeve's Tale takes the idea of "quitting" and puts it center stage, changing altogether the dynamic of the first fragment. As the Knight's Tale was "repaid" and "replayed" in the Miller's Tale (both about two men in love with the same woman) on a different status level, and as the Miller parodied and highlighted the idealized nature of the Knight's Tale by replacing its romance setting with gritty realism, so the Reeve's Tale performs a similar treatment on the Miller's.

It is clear from the moment that the angry Reeve quietly fumes among all the jollity after the Miller's Tale that he is of rather a severe disposition, and there is nothing of the warmth and good humor of the Miller's Tale: there is no sign of an elaborate, enjoyable fabliau trick like Nicholas' elaborate (and, when you consider that John the Miller goes out to the country regularly anyway, rather unnecessary) plan. What the Reeve narrates is brutal, animal, copulation:

> Withinne a while this John the clerk up leep,

And on this goode wyf he leith on soore.

So myrie a fit ne hadde she nat ful yore;

He priketh harde and depe as he were mad.

(4228-31)

There is a harder, more vengeful quality to this "quitting" tale, and, again, our attention is drawn to the anger of the teller in the Canterbury framework – how far does the bile of the vengeful Reeve seep into the telling of the story as Chaucer repeats it to us? Larry Benson supposes the Reeve's Tale, like the Miller's, based directly on a French fabliau, since two surviving fabliaux offer close parallels to Chaucer's story, and yet the tone of the tale is quite different from that of the

Miller's.

What the Reeve's Tale undoubtedly demonstrates is Seth Lerer's observation that language becomes gradually broken down, gradually devalued as the first fragment progresses. Where the Knight's courtly, formal language descended to the bodily noises of the Miller's Tale, language in the Reeve's Tale seems replaced altogether for the most part - by action. Symkyn's wife and daughter are not persuaded into bed, or even seduced slightly, but just leapt upon. The denouement of the tale is a dumbshow played out in the dark: silent sex, moving cradles, and, eventually a brawl involving most of the participants on the floor. The graceful, formal, rhetoric of Theseus' "First Mover" speech already seems a long way away.

Note too that no-one - and this is different even to the Miller's Tale - actually does any verbal persuading in words in the Reeve's Tale. The plot of the tale consists largely of moving things around: beginning with the release of the clerks' horse, followed by the hiding of their loaf of bread by the Miller, and then, of course, the various movements of the cradle at the bottom of the bed. Instead of words, we have another form of signification, in which objects carry certain meanings. The cradle, for example, (a neat symbol, considering what happens in the bed it delineates!) is used to dictate which bed is the miller's and which not. The meaning and the value of words and speaking is central to the Tales as a whole - and language in The Knight's Tale became verbal exclamations in The Miller's Tale, and, in The Reeve's Tale, is replaced by simple, physical signposts.

Note too that the two clerks speak in a Northern dialect of Middle English, which might be seen to disintegrate the formality of the language even further: Chaucer, of course, claiming to repeat exactly the words in which someone told the tale, meticulously transcribes the dialect into the direct speech of the clerks.

"The feend is on me falle" (4288) the miller's wife cries out as the miller trips and falls onto her, and the idea of a fall – from grace, from the ceiling in a kneading trough, or from a horse – is key to the final twists of each of the Canterbury Tales told thus far. In a more metaphorical sense, too, we can see that the idea of man's fall from paradise is replayed to some extent in the move from the romantic Knight's Tale to the bawdy, human tales of the Miller and Reeve: it is a post-lapserian, "real" world we are presented with.

One final question is the question of justice. How far is the justice delivered on Symkyn deserved – how far is it funny, how far a necessary justice, and how far is it trickery gone too far? Symkyn is struck out cold by his wife at the end of the tale, and yet Chaucer carefully includes the detail of the clerks beating him even when he lies unconscious. Do we laugh at this, or recoil from it? Whose side are we on? Deceivers will be deceived: bad people should not expect good things, the Reeve tells us as his moral. But this simplistic justice doesn't play out so simply within his tale: and the subversion and complication of ideas of justice will only continue through the Tales as a whole.

Summary and Analysis of The Cook's Tale

The Cook's Prologue

Roger of Ware, the Cook, claps the Reeve on the back "for joye". Delighted with the way Symkyn the miller had received his comeuppance in the tale, the Cook then promises a tale of his own, despite the fact that he is only a "povre man" (a poor man). The Host answers, granting Roger the next tale. But he adds "looke that it be good", and comments on Roger's tendency to draw the gravy out of unsold pies, and resell pies that have already been reheated twice in his shop, full of flies.

The Host's conclusion incites Roger the Cook to tell a story "in game" (in jest, in fun).. Roger agrees, and, reminding Harry Bailly (the Host) not to be angry, particularly because his tale is about a "hostileer" (pub-owner, like the Host himself), he begins his tale.

The Cook's Tale

Once an apprentice lived in "our city" (perhaps "Ware" in Hertfordshire – the town the Cook is from) and his craft was selling food. He was a short man, with a dark complexion and black hair – and he was an excellent dancer: so good, that people called him "Perkin Reveller" (to "revel" is to dance and have a good time).

He loved the tavern better than his shop, and, whenever there was a procession in Cheapside, he would run out of the shop to enjoy himself and dance, forgetting about work. He often stole from his master, with whom he lived until he had finished his apprenticeship. However, one day, his master sent for him, and quoting the proverb "It is better to take the rotten apple out of the bag than to have it rot all the other apples", decided to get rid of him.

Now this jolly apprentice had his leave, and could riot all night if he so pleased – and eventually, he found board with a companion of his own sort: who loved dice, and reveling, and pleasure. This companion had a wife who, for the sake of appearances only, kept a shop – and had sex for a living. Thus – abruptly – ends the Cook's Tale.

Analysis

Thus ends the first fragment of the Canterbury Tales with a tale that breaks off before it has really gets anywhere - and the real question is whether the tale is deliberately left unfinished by Chaucer, whether he intended to return to it, or whether we have just lost some of the manuscript. There are no definite answers, unfortunately, and critics have argued for all three positions.

That said, there are a few interesting things about the tale as we have it. Firstly, Roger of Ware seems to have been a real person who lived at the same time as Chaucer. This lends a whole new aspect to the Canterbury Tales, if we consider that Chaucer might have populated his pilgrimage with real people, whom his audience might have recognized. The whole question, raised already in other tales, of reality verses fiction, takes on a deeper level when we consider that Chaucer is not the only pilgrim to have a dual existence - in the real world and within the fictional one. Might this tale be in some way a parody or a joke at the real Roger's expense? It's very possible, but impossible to prove.

Seth Lerer has persuasively argued that – like many other of Chaucer's works, including "The House of Fame", and "The Legend of Good Women" – there is a very real possibility that the Cook's Tale might have been left deliberately unfinished. It is, Professor Lerer argues, a tale which breaks off just at the point where we understand what sort of tale it is to be – a grim, gritty tale about a prostitute and a drunken, good-for-nothing apprentice. The trajectory from the formal, fictionalized, stylish romance of the Knight's Tale, down through the fabliaux of the Miller and Reeve hits rock-bottom with a realistic tale about a real Cook and animal copulation in exchange for money. We don't hear the Cook's Tale told: but we know all too well what sort of thing is to come next - and so language disintegrates completely at the end of the First Fragment. Formal language was replaced by bodily noises in the Miller's Tale, language was replaced by action in the Reeve's Tale, and now language stops altogether. The whole project of the Tales comes to a dead standstill.

Summary and Analysis of The Man of Law's Tale

Introduction to The Man of Law's Tale

The Host, realizing that time is moving on, reminds the pilgrims that, while lost cattle can be found, lost time never returns. Addressing the Man of Law (a lawyer, in modern terms) in a mock-legal way, the Host asks him to tell the next tale, and "stonden in this cas at my juggement" (a joke, for the Host, of course, is to judge which tale is the best).

"Host", the Man of Law, replies, "To breke forward is nat myn entente", and reiterating that he does not break agreements, agrees to tell the tale. But, the Man of Law continues, "I kan right now no thrifty tale seyn" (I have no suitable tale now to tell [say]), because Chaucer – excellent at metre and at coming up with clever rhymes – has already told them all in one book or another. The Man of Law then recites a little list of Chaucer's (actual!) works so far: Ceyx and Alcione (in *The Book of the Duchess*), and the Legend of Good Women – noting that Chaucer has never told a tale about wicked Canacee, who sinfully had an incestuous relationship with her own brother. Nor will the Man of Law tell a tale about her either.

"I speke in prose", the Man of Law continues, juxtaposing himself with the poet, Chaucer, and then with a good cheer begins his tale.

The Prologue of The Man of Law's Tale

The Prologue begins by lamenting the condition of poverty; it makes a person steal, beg or borrow for money, it makes a person blame Christ, and it makes a person jealous of his neighbor. If you are poor, the Prologue continues, your brother hates you, and all your friends fly from your side. The Prologue then finally addresses "rich marchauntz", who are always happy, because they are always rich – before the Man of Law's personal voice seems to segue in, adding that he would be without a tale to tell, had he not heard a tale from a merchant, many years ago.

The Man of Law's Tale

(I)

In Syria there dwelt a company of wealthy traders who made a journey to Rome. After a certain time there, they heard of the beauty of Constance, the emperor's daughter, renowned equally for her virtue, her goodness and her beauty. When they had seen her themselves, the merchants returned to Syria, and reported to the sultan, who was immediately taken with lust and wonder for Constance.

The sultan met with his advisors and told them of his intent, but they could conceive of no way that he could marry Constance, for no Christian emperor would allow his daughter to marry a Muslim. "Rather than I lese / Custance, I wol be cristned" (Rather than I lose / Constance, I will be christened) answered the sultan, and, insisting that his baronage were christened with him, the sultan set about having his court christened.

The Roman Emperor heard of the sultan's desire, and agreed to it, organizing a huge amount of pomp and circumstance for the occasion. The day arrived for Constance to depart, and everyone prepared themselves. But Constance, overcome with sorrow, arose from bed and dressed to depart, knowing that there was no other way things could be.

It is no wonder, the narrator comments, that she wept, considering that she was being sent to a foreign country, away from her friends, to be married to someone she had never met. Constance then addressed her father, sad to leave him and go to the "Barbre nacioun" (pagan land), hoping that she would fulfill Christ's behest, continuing

> I, wrecche woman, no fors though I spille! (I am just a wretched woman, and it doesn't matter if I die)

Wommen are born to thralldom and penance, (women are born to slavery and suffering)

And to been under mannes governance. (and to live under men's governing)

Constance was brought to the ship, and desperately trying to put on a brave face, sailed away.

Meanwhile, the Sultan's mother, "welle of vices" (a well of vice), who knew her son's intention, called her counsellers to her and told them that she would rather die than renounce Mohammed's law (and Islam). Each man swore to live and die with her, and she instructed them to be baptized as her son had ordered ("Cooold water shal nat greve us but a lite!")

The first part of the tale ends with a damning of the Sultanesse, the "roote of iniquitee", as the Sultan agrees to do her the honor of having the Christians to feast at her table.

(II)

The Christians arrived in Syria with a great and solemn crowd, and, after many celebrations, the time came for all of the Christian folk, along with the Sultan's entourage, to feast at the Sultanesse's house. The tale breaks off to mourn "sodeyn wo, that evere art successour / To worldly blisse" (sudden woe, which is always the successor of worldly bliss) before revealing that every one of the Christians and the Sultan were knifed and cut to pieces at the table. There was now in Syria no-one who had converted to Christianity – only Constance survived.

The Sultanesse's men took Constance and put her in a ship without a rudder, bidding her to learn to sail out of Syria and back to Italy. She had a certain amount of treasure on board, and the men had supplied her with food and with clothes - and forth she sailed across the sea. Constance blessed herself and said a prayer to Christ's cross. At this point the story breaks back to narrative again, and the Man of Law (or Chaucer) raises the question of why Constance was not also killed at the feast – answering it with another question: who saved Daniel in the lion's den? Christian God is the answer to both.

The ship finally crashed on the shores of Northumberland. The warden of a nearby castle found Constance and gave her shelter, but she refused to reveal her identity. He and his wife, Dame Hermengyld, were pagans, but Constance soon secretly converted the wife to Christianity. In this heathen land, Christians could only practice their faith in secret. While walking on the beach, Constance, Hermengyld and her husband came upon a blind Christian, who identified her without his eyes. Although Hermengild feared that her husband would reproach her for attempting the conversion, this miracle converted him too to Christianity.

The warden was not the lord of the castle. Instead, it was Alla, the king of Northumberland. A young knight, influenced by Satan, fell in love with Constance, but she would not return her favors. In an attempt to exact revenge upon her, he broke into the bedchamber where Constance and Dame Hermengyld slept, slit Hermengyld's throat and placed the knife beside Constance. Soon after the warden came home with Alla and found his wife murdered. Taking her before King Alla, who was told all the circumstances of Constance's arrival in Northumberland, the false knight (who killed Hermengyld) insisted that Constance had done the murder.

The people spoke out on her behalf, unable to believe that Constance had done the crime; and this provoked the king to inquire further into the circumstances of what had happened. Constance fell to her knees and prayed, looking around her for help. "Now hastily do fecche a book", King Alla commanded, deciding that, if the knight swore on the book that Constance was responsible, he would think carefully about his decision. A book was brought, and, the knight swore on it that Constance was guilty - at that time, a hand struck him down on the neck-bone, and he fell down like a stone, both of his eyes bursting out of his face.

Witnessing this miracle, the king – "and many another in that place" – was converted to Christianity., and decided to take Constance for his wife. But, who was upset about this wedding but Donegild, the knight's mother? She thought her heart had broken in two. In the meantime, the couple were wedded, and Constance gave birth to a boy, named Mauricius, while Alla was away in Scotland fighting. A messenger, taking the news to the king, was forestalled by the queen who insisted he stayed with her that night, and, while he was asleep, replaced his letters with forged ones. Her letters claimed that Constance's baby was foul and wicked; and when Alla wrote back that he vowed to love the child regardless, Donegild replaced his letter with an order to banish Constance and her child from the land on the same boat from which they came.

(III)

When Alla returned home, he learned what had happened and murdered his mother for her cruelty, and for being a traitor. But Constance had already set sail, and washed up in another heathen land, where the warden's steward came on board her ship, telling her that he would be her lover whether she liked it or not. Her child cried, and Constance cried also; but the Virgin Mary came to her aid, and, in the struggle that ensued, the steward fell overboard and drowned in the sea.

Returning to Syria, the emperor of Rome had sent an army, hearing of the slaughter of Christians by the sultaness, and, having burnt, slain and avenged themselves on the heathen people, this army was now returning homeward to Rome. The senator in charge of the army met Constance in her ship, and, not knowing who she was, brought her home to Rome, where she stayed for a "longe tyme".

King Alla, having slain his mother, had come to Rome to receive his penance and seek Christ's forgiveness for the wickedness he had performed. The rumor spread through Rome of how Alla was to come in pilgrimage, and this senator came to do him reverence. Constance's son went in the entourage of the senator to feast with King Alla.

The child stood at the feast, looking into the king's face; Alla then asked the senator whose the child was. "A mooder he hath", replied the senator, "but fader hath he noon", and told him the story of how the child was found. Remembering Constance's face, and seeing the resemblance in her child's face, Alla sped from the table as soon as he could, debating with himself about the hallucination he thought he was having. But afterwards, the senator sent for Constance, and, when Alla saw his wife, he wept, because it had come true. Constance stood as dumb as a tree, stiff with emotion, when she remembered his unkindness: which he soon explained had not been of his doing. When all was explained, they kissed a hundred times, and were blissfully happy.

The Emperor had granted that King Alla could dine with him; and, as she saw her father in the street, Constance laid down at his needs, and explained to him who she was. There was such joy between the three of them that it cannot be described.

Later, Constance's child Maurice was made Emperor by the Pope, but, the narrator reiterates, "Of Custance is my tale specially". Constance and Alla came to England to live in joy and in peace, but sadly, only a year after they had been reunited, Death took King Alla from the world. Constance, at the very end of the tale, widowed, makes her way again to Rome, to find her father and praise God.

Epilogue to the Man of Law's Tale

"This was a thrify tale for the nones!" proclaims the Host, happy with the Man of Law's tale, before turning to the "Parisshe Priest" to tell the next tale. The Parson then rebukes the Host for swearing blasphemously, only to be mocked in turn by the Host as a "Jankin" (a derisive name for a priest) and a "Lollard" (a heretic). The Host, announcing that the "Lollard" will do some preaching, is interrupted by the Shipman, who objects to the idea of the Parson glossing the gospel and teaching. He promises a tale which will "clynk" like a merry bell, and wake up all the company. But, the Shipman continues, there will be no philosophy or legal matters in his tale (unlike in the Man of Laws) – "ther is but litel Latyn in my mawe!" (there is only a little bit of Latin in my stomach").

Analysis

There's another moment at the very start of the Man of Law's Prologue, in which the boundary between fiction and reality once again seems extremely blurred: the "Geffrey Chaucer" who exists as a character on the Canterbury pilgrimage is ascribed the bibliography of the Chaucer we are reading by the Man of Law, who cites works we know that the "real" Chaucer actually wrote. Once again, the Tales pretend to a real, documentary status, as if they are dramatizing or merely reporting word for word true events, and real people – and our narrator, Chaucer, seems to elide the fictional world with the reader's world.

The Man of Law, then, a "lawyer" is someone concerned with the laws and rules that hold in place the real world, and – at least, so the General Prologue tells us – he knows by heart all the lines of the common law: "every statu koude he pleyn by rote". Carolyn Dinshaw, the excellent feminist critic, has written that the Man of Law is indeed "of law", made up of law, his head filled up with laws; and moreover, she reads the tale of Constance as asserting the status quo of Chaucer's world at the time the tale was written.

Women, Dinshaw argues, were a matter of business in the middle ages, and – particularly as the marriage of a daughter could produce a strong link between two merchants or families – children were an important financial asset. Constance, then, first appearing in the tale as a tale told by merchants, is effectively sold forth by her father; the marriage is actually dealt with as if it were a business deal. The Prologue to the tale tells us that the Man of Law even heard this tale from a merchant: and it is not a huge leap to make from the business of merchants, trading goods back and forward across the sea, to Constance, sent from Rome to Syria, to Northumberland, to another heathen land, and eventually back to Rome. Constance, in other words, serves as "goods", saleable, valuable, and whose value, appropriately, remains constant.

Dinshaw then relates the tale as a whole to that end of the Chaucer bibliography the Man of Law recites in the prologue: the final lines where he disdains to tell a tale concerning incest. The Man of Law's Tale is indeed full of contradictions: in Dinshaw's words

> "He promises to tell a tale in prose, for example, but instead we get a poem in rime royal. The "poverte" Prologue seems to have only the barest, most expedient relation to the Tale itself.... Most puzzling of them all is the Man of Law's specific insistence, on the one hand, that he will not tell a tale of incest, and his choice, on the other hand, of a narrative whose motivation in well-known analogues is, in fact, incest..."

(Carolyn Dinshaw, *Chaucer's Sexual Poetics*, p.88)

The critic Margaret Schlauch has suggested persuasively that in all of the sources to the Man of Law's tale, Constance's father makes sexual demands upon his daughter, and Dinshaw wonders whether Constance might be escaping from a father with incestuous desires. What, we might ask, is the relevance of this incest theme to the idea of Constance as a mercantile pawn?

Levi-Strauss has the answer. If marriage (and the marital sex it makes permissible) is a pawn in a merchant's transaction, and the social order is maintained through trading women and trading marriage, then forbidding incest is the best way to maintain that order. For a daughter – a father's mercantile asset – is no longer an asset in circulation if the father sleeps with her himself. Incest breaks down the idea of a woman as something to be traded: breaks down, in short, the law.

Dinshaw's interpretation is a fascinating one, and one which ties together the prologue and the tale, as well as some of the key notions explored about female identity in the Tales: (i) the idea of the woman as something to be traded, as merchandise, (ii) the idea of a patriarchal society keen to keep women "in circulation", and (iii) the idea of the woman as duplicitous and evil, as presented by the two malicious mothers. What it misses, however, is the over-riding religious nature of the tale; and the good fortune visited on Constance (herself, literally a child of Rome) for maintaining her Christian faith.

Yet Constance is not simply merchandise. Chaucer's – and the Man of Law's tale – also keeps "Constance", (or "a Constance", in precisely the way that "Geffrey" is "a Chaucer") in circulation; within the context of the tale-telling game, it uses Constance's story as a potential avenue for profit. There is an interesting moment early in the first part of the tale when Constance is described as "pale", as if, pre-marriage, she is white, blank, hardly visible. The tale itself dresses Constance - clothes her, and makes her palatable to an audience in order to exchange her - and remember that "text", "textile" and "cloth" (a major piece of merchandise in the Middle Ages) have shared linguistic roots.

Perhaps part of the reason that the tale is the "Man of Law's" and not the "Lawyer's" is precisely to emphasize the fact that Constance, exchanged by men for profit within the tale, is also being exchanged by a **Man** within the tale-telling framework. The Man of Law and Chaucer, by writing Constance's story, contribute to the way she is exchanged and re-presented as a feminine symbol within it. Writing a woman is to make her the creation of a man; an idea worth emphasizing before the next tale – the Wife of Bath's, which takes this idea several stages further - begins.

Summary and Analysis of The Wife of Bath's Tale

Prologue to the Wife of Bath's Tale

"Experience", even if no written authorities existed in the world, "is right ynogh for me". Thus begins the voice of the Wife of Bath. She has certainly had "experience", and is keen to justify it against biblical authority. She has had five husbands and justifies it in scripture: Christ never taught that people should only be married once, the Bible says "go forth and multiply", and Solomon had more than one wife. The Wife's husbands, picked out by their "chestes" and "nether purs", have all been good men, and she is looking forward to the sixth. She also points out that Jesus never lays down a law about virginity, and essentially states that we have the parts for sex and should use them as such: "they were nat maad for noght".

Scripture, the Wife points out, can be interpreted "bothe up and doun" – you can argue that genitals are for purgation of urine, or to tell the female from the male, and for nothing else. The Wife then states again that she will "use myn instrument" whenever her husband decides he wants to "paye his dette". Her husband, the Wife continues, shall be both her "dettour and my thral" (debtor and slave) and that she would mark it on his flesh.

At this point, the Pardoner interrupts, claiming he was about to marry a wife and that the Wife has put him off – and she advises him to listen to her tale before making a judgement, and looks like beginning it, before going off on another tangent, silencing the Pardoner altogether.

Three of the Wife's husbands were good, and two were bad: the three were good, rich and old (and impotent!) and they gave the Wife all their land, which resulted in her withholding sex from them in order to get exactly what she wanted. Women, the Wife continues, can lie and steal better than any man. She reveals her tactic for manipulating her husbands – deliberately attacking her husband with a whole fistful of complaints and several biblical glossing (for justification) and starting an argument, with the result of her getting what she wants. By accusing her husband of infidelity, the Wife disguised her own adultery – even calling her maid and Jankin in false witness to back her up.

The Wife also got money out of her husbands by claiming that, if she were to sell her "bele chose" (sexual favours), she would make more money than they lavished on her. Thus the Wife treated her first three husbands, the three, good, old, rich men. The Wife's fourth husband was a reveler and had a mistress as well as a wife. He was a match for the Wife of Bath, sharing some of her qualities, but he soon died.

The fifth husband was the most cruel to her: kind in bed but otherwise violent, beating her viciously. He could "glose" (gloss – persuade – flatter) her extremely well when he wanted to have sex, and she loved him best, because he played hard to get with her. He had been a student at Oxford, and came to be a boarder at the home of the Wife's best friend, Alison, while she was still married to husband number four. Soon after he died, she married Jankin (number five) who was, at twenty, exactly half the Wife's age.

Very regularly, Jankin read his book of "wikked wyves", a compilation volume of anti-feminist literature, containing works from Valerius and Theophrastus, St. Jerome, Tertullian, Solomon, and many others. The Wife interrupts herself to express her anger at the anti-feminist portrayals of women in books written by male clerks – and wishes that women "hadde written stories" like clerks have, in order to redress balance. Then, her story continues: Jankin was reading aloud from his book by the fire, and the Wife, fed up that he would never finish reading his "cursed book al nyght", tore out three pages, punching him in the face so that he fell backward into the fire. Jankin got up fast and hit her on the head with his fist, knocking her to the floor, where she lay as if dead. "Hastow slayn me, false theef?" the Wife bellow when she awoke, "and for my land thus hastow mordred me?" (Have you killed me, false thief? And have you murdered me to get my land?"). Jankin, of course, then begged her forgiveness; and the Wife made him burn his book right there.

Having gained for herself all of the "maistrie" (mastery, control, dominance), Jankin then begged her to keep all of her own land, and – after that day – they never argued again. The Wife was true to him, and he to her, and she was extremely generous to him. At this point, the Wife announces again that she is to tell her tale.

The words between the Summoner and the Friar

The Friar laughs to hear everything that the Wife has said, commenting that it is a "long preamble of a tale" (a long prologue to a tale) – and when the Summoner hears the Friar's voice, he attacks him, commenting that friars are notorious for their long-windedness, telling him to "go sit doun!". The Friar promises, in revenge, to tell a tale about a summoner to make everyone laugh. The Host quiets them down, and encourages the Wife to tell her tale.

The Wife of Bath's Tale

The Wife of Bath's Tale tells a story from a distant time, when King Arthur ruled the nation and when elves used to run around impregnating women. However, the Wife immediately digresses: now friars have taken the place of elves - they are now the copulating, evil spirits.

King Arthur had a knight who, when riding home one day from hawking, found a maiden walking alone and raped her. This crime usually held the penalty of death, but, in court, the queen intervened and begged her husband to spare the knight, promising the knight that she would grant his life if he could answer the question "What do women most desire?" She gave him one year to find the answer.

The knight went on a journey but could find no satisfactory answer; some said wealth, others jollity, some status, others a good lover in bed. Despondent that he might not find his answer, the knight was mournful, when, riding beside a forest on his way back to his home, he saw a dance of twenty-four ladies. Approaching them, they vanished, and in their place, the knight found a hideous old woman, the "lothly lady", to whom he put his question. She agreed to give the answer and assured him that it was the right one, but would only tell him the answer if he would do the next thing that she required of him. When the knight agreed, she whispered in his ear.

When they arrived at court, the knight faced the queen again, and told him that women desired to have sovereignty and "to been in maistrie" (to be in mastery) above their husbands. The lothly lady then spoke up before the court, announcing the knight's pledge, and asking him to take her for his wife. The knight, although now pardoned, was miserable that he had to marry such an old crone, but there was no way for him to get out of it.

Privately, the knight wedded the lothly lady the next day, and the two of them lay in bed. She realized his unhappiness, and confronted him about it. He criticized her for not only being old and ugly, but low-born. She scoffed at his snobbery as a definition and defended her poverty as irrelevant to God. She then gave him a choice, making him see both sides of the argument. Either he could have her as an old and ugly wife who would be entirely faithful to him; or he could have her as a young and fair wife, who would probably cuckold him.

The knight sighed sorely, and thought, but finally told his wife to choose herself whichever option would bring most honor to the two of them. "Thanne have I gete of yow maistrie" (In that case, I've got mastery over you) she said – and the knight agreed that she had. The lothly lady asked him to kiss her and "cast up the curtyn" (lift up the curtain) to look on her face – she had transformed into a young and beautiful woman. They lived happily ever after: and, the Wife concludes, let Christ grant all women submissive husbands who sexually satisfy their wives, and let Christ kill all men who will not be governed by their wives.

Analysis

The Wife of Bath is one of Chaucer's most enduring characters, and rightly, one of the most famous of any of the Canterbury pilgrims. Her voice is extremely distinctive – loud, self-promoting, extremely aggressive – and her lengthy prologue silences the Pardoner and the Friar (who is then parodied at the start of the Tale) for daring to interrupt her. One of the key issues for interpreting the Wife's tale historically has been the relationship between prologue and tale: some critics have found in the Wife's fairy-tale ending a wistful, saddened dreaminess from an elderly woman whose hopes for a sixth husband might turn out to be futile. Other critics have treated the tale as a matter of "maistrie" and control, arguing that the Wife's tale, starting as it does with a rape (a man physically dominating a woman), is deeply ambiguous at its close about precisely whose desire is being fulfilled. Surely there is little point in the woman having the maistrie if all she is to do with it is to please her husband?

Yet it seems to me that the Wife's tale and prologue can be treated as one lengthy monologue, and it is the voice we attribute **that** monologue too which proves impossible to precisely define. The Wife's tale inherits the issue of the woman as literary text (Constance, in the Man of Law's tale, was "pale", like paper waiting to be written on, and used as an exchangeable currency by the merchants and – perhaps – by the Man of Law) and develops it.

Text, and the interpretation of text is absolutely central to the Wife of Bath's Tale. The General Prologue describes her as being swathed in textile, and, of course, "textere", the Latin verb meaning "to weave" is the key to a close relationship between "cloth" and "text" in the Middle Ages. For the Wife, as well as being excellent at spinning a tale, is also excellent at spinning cloth – and is surrounded, problematically in text in just the way the Prologue has her covered in cloth. When, at the very end of her tale, the lothly lady implores her husband to "cast up the curtyn" and see her as she really is, she highlights one of the key problems in the tale: it is very difficult to ascertain precisely where fiction stops and reality begins.

The Wife claims to represent female voices – and her tale consists of a set of women representing each other. The raped maiden is represented by the queen, who in turn is represented by the lothly lady, who in turn becomes a beautiful lady: the image which precedes her appearance is, appropriately, twenty four ladies apparently vanishing into one. The Wife speaks on behalf of women everywhere: and against the male clerks who have written the antifeminist literature that Jankin reads in his book of wikked wyves.

It is odd then, that the Wife, who claims to stand for "experience", spends much of her prologue dealing with written "authority", glossing the Bible in precisely the manner she criticizes the clerks for doing. The Wife is against text, but expert in text; against clerks, but particularly clerical; and, of course, venomous about anti-feminist literature, but also made up of anti-feminist literature. When the Wife throws Jankin's book in the fire, she is in fact burning her own sources (Jerome, Theophrastus et. al) which constitutes a bizarre act of literary self-orphanage. It is as if she burns her own birth certificate.

When you notice too that the Wife (whose name is Alison) has as her only confidant another woman called Alison, there is an unusual sense that she might be talking only to herself. Add to that her almost uninterrupted monologue of tale and prologue – and the almost-uninterrupted monologues of Jankin (reading from the book of wives) and the lothly lady's lengthy monologue on poverty and gentilesse – and you see that, in fact, the voice of the Wife does indeed take the "maistrie" in the tale itself. It entirely dominates the tale.

The Wife, then, is a far more complicated figure than simply a proto-feminist. She asks the key question herself: "Who peynted the leon, tel me who?", referring to the old myth that, a lion, seeing the picture of a man triumphing over a lion, asked the rhetorical question which pointed out that the portrayal was biased as it had been painted by a man, not a lion. If the Wife's tale is a depiction of a woman triumphing over a man (and even that is not easy to decide) can it be similarly dismissed?

Perhaps. But of course, for all the Wife decries the clerical tradition and the clerks who leave out the good deeds of woman, she herself as a text is another example of a lecherous, lying, manipulative woman. She falls into the anti-feminist tradition she represents. This is even before you mention that the Wife is being written, at the very least ventriloquised, by Geoffrey Chaucer, a clerk and a man. Is this Chaucer's opinion of proto-feminism and a disavowal of the anti-feminist tradition? Or is Chaucer endorsing the anti-feminist tradition by giving it a mouthpiece which, in arguing against it, demonstrates all of its stereotypical arguments as fact?

Who painted the lion? Whose voice is the Wife's? Is she worthy of – as she does – speaking for women everywhere?

These are all huge, open, fascinating questions that demonstrate why the tale itself is so complex, and interesting to interpret. The key fact not to forget is that you can't have a Wife without a Husband. Whether married to Chaucer, whether Chaucer in drag, or whether a feminist persona all of her own, it's important to view the apparently proto-feminist Wife of Bath from a point of view which understands her strong links to the men in her fictional – and literary – lives.

Summary and Analysis of The Friar's Tale

Prologue to the Friar's Tale

The Friar commends the Wife of Bath for her tale, and then says, in line with his promise between the Wife's Prologue and Tale, that he will tell a tale about a summoner. He does not wish to offend the Summoner who travels with them, but insists that summoners are known for fornication and lewd behavior. The Summoner, on the surface at least, does not take offense, but does indicate that he will "quit" the Friar in turn. The job of a summoner, to which the Friar objects, is to issue summons from the church against sinners who, under penalty of excommunication, pay indulgences for their sins to the church, a sum which illicit summoners often pocket. The Host quiets the argument down, and the Friar's Tale begins.

The Friar's Tale

The Friar's Tale tells of an archdeacon who boldly carried out the Church's laws against fornication, witchcraft and lechery. Lechers received the greatest punishment, forced to pay significant tithes to the church. The archdeacon had a summoner who was quite adept at discovering lechers, even though he himself was immoral. Friars, the Friar says, are out of the jurisdiction of summoners, and at this point, the Summoner interrupts the Friar's Tale, disagreeing. The Host allows the Friar to continue his tale, and he immediately continues to attack summoners.

The summoner of the Friar's Tale would only summon those who had enough money to pay the church, and would take half the charge himself: he was a thief, and a bawd, enlisting the help of prostitutes who would reveal their customers to the summoner in exchange for their own safety (and offer of sexual services).

One day, the summoner was traveling to issue a summons to an old widow, when he met a yeoman on the way, dressed in a green jacket. The summoner claimed to be a bailiff, knowing that his actual profession was so detested. The yeoman offered hospitality to the summoner. The two travelled together, and the summoner asked where the yeoman lived, intending to later rob him of the gold and silver he claimed to possess. The summoner asks the yeoman how he makes money at his job, and the yeoman admits that he lives by extortion and theft; and the summoner admits that he does the same.

The two reveal to each other their villainy, until the yeoman finally declares that he is a fiend whose dwelling is in hell. The summoner asks the yeoman (the devil) why he has a human shape, and he replies that he assumes one whenever on earth. The summoner asks him why he is on earth, receiving the reply that sometimes devils are God's instruments. The devil claims that the summoner will meet him again someday and have better evidence of hell than Dante or Virgil. The summoner suggests that the two continue on their way and go about their business, each taking their share.

On their travels they found a carter whose wagon, loaded with hay, was stuck in the mud. "The devel have al, bothe hors and cart and hey!" cursed the carter, and the summoner, taking the carter literally, implored the devil to take all of the carter's belongings. The devil comments that, although that is what he is literally saying, that is not what the carter means: "the carl spak oo thing, but he thoghte another". On the devil's encouragement, the carter prays to God, and, lo and behold, the horses pull the wagon from the mud.

The summoner suggests that they visit the widow he was originally visiting. On arriving, the summoner gives her a notice to appear before the archdeacon on the penalty of excommunication, but she claims that she is sick and cannot travel there. She asks if she can pay the summoner to represent her to the archdeacon, and he demands twelve pence, a sum that she thinks is too great, for, she claims, she is guiltless of sin. The summoner then demands her new pan from her, claiming that he paid her fine for making her husband a cuckold (an accusation which she expressly denies). She curses the summoner, saying that she gives his body to the devil. The devil hears this and tells the summoner that he shall be in hell tonight. Upon these words, the summoner and the devil disappeared into hell, the realm where summoners truly belong.

Analysis:

The pattern of reciprocity and "quitting", as seen in the Miller's and Reeve's tale in the First Fragment, is reintroduced with the Friar's and Summoner's tale. These two would likely be, to Chaucer's readers, easily recognizable characters, and the rapacious clergyman was very much a stock figure for Middle English readers and listeners.

The Friar's Tale, like the Reeve's Tale, seems to exist for a single purpose: the humiliation and degradation of members of a certain profession. The Tale begins by exposing the means by which summoners blackmail and extort persons, but does not attack the church system that allows this to happen, but rather the men who represent this system and exploit these workings of the church. Yet the Friar's Tale surpasses the Reeve's Tale in its vitriol for its main character. While Symkyn, the immoral miller of the Reeve's tale, is hardly an exemplary character and exists only for ridicule, he at least is given a proper name that separates him from his profession. The main character of the Friar's Tale is an impersonal representation of all summoners and the fate they deserve.

The comic twist to the Friar's Tale is that, when he meets the devil, the summoner is neither shocked nor overcome with fear. Rather, the summoner regards the devil as a curious colleague, and is almost impressed. In fact, the narrator too seems to hold a higher opinion of the devil than of the summoner. When the devil leaves the summoner, the devil tells him that they shall hold company together until he forsakes him. This may be a chance for redemption that the devil offers the summoner , just before he visits the old crone, but he does not take it.

Of course, as well as preaching against hypocrisy, the Friar's Tale turns it into a plot feature. How can we know, the tale asks, who we meet on the road: a yeoman or a devil? A religious, pious summoner, or a downright crook? Moreover, there is nothing very ambiguous about the ending to the tale: the summoner is taken to hell. A metaphorical hell, like the furnace of Gervase the smith in the Miller's Tale, is a far more distant representation, but when the summoner disappears, with Satan, it is simply, unmetaphorically, to hell. What in the Miller's tale was comedy, when stated literally by the Friar, starts to look a little like blasphemy, and one wonders how easily Chaucer's original readers would have related to it.

Penn R. Szittya has written, in his essay "The Green Yeoman as Loathly Lady: The Friar's Parody of the Wife of Bath's Tale", that the Friar's Tale might actually be a parody of the Wife of Bath's tale. Szittya notes such pertinent details as the appearance of the Friar riding "under a forest syde" - in precisely the same phrase that the Wife uses in her tale - and argues that the Wife's fairytale forest, and the Friar's real one in some way elide. It is difficult however to be entirely persuaded by Szittya's argument, and see the Friar's tale as a closer relation to the Wife's than it is to the Summoner's.

Simply put, the Friar's tale is also a reminder to watch what you wish for, and not to speak without thinking. The devil, it seems, takes words literally - and whether you mean them or not, can decide to act upon them as he pleases, as long as they have been uttered (note the way the widow's curse is made reality by the devil as the tale resolves). As Chaucer's Tales look perilously close to potential blasphemy, the Friar's Tale's warning that anything said can be used against the sayer seems doubly pertinent; and the issue of blasphemy in the Tales, present here, runs right through the work to Chaucer's final Retraction.

Summary and Analysis of The Summoner's Tale

Prologue to the Summoner's Tale

The Summoner was enraged by the tale that the Friar told, quaking in anger. Since, he says, you have all listened to the Friar lie, please do listen to my tale. The Summoner claims that friars and fiends are one and the same. He tells a short anecdote in his prologue. One day, a friar was brought to hell and led up and down by angel, and was surprised to see no friars there. Are friars so graceful, he asked, that they never come to hell? The angel told him that many millions of friars came to hell, and led him directly to Satan. Satan had a tail as broad as a sailing ship, and the angel called to Satan to lift up his tail. Satan did, and twenty thousand friars swarmed out of his arse like bees from a hive.

The Summoner's Tale

A friar went to preach and beg in a marshy region of Yorkshire called Holderness. In his sermons he begged for donations for the church and afterward he begged for charity from the local residents. The Friar interrupts, calling the Summoner a liar, but is silenced by the Host.

Along went this friar, house by house, until he came to the house of Thomas, a local resident who normally indulged him, and found him ill. The friar spoke of the sermon he had given that day, commenting on the excellent way he had glossed the biblical text (and making the famous comment that "Glosynge is a glorious thyng") - and essentially ordered a meal from Thomas's wife.

She told the friar that her child died not more than two weeks before. The friar claimed that he had a revelation that her child had died and entered heaven. He claimed that his fellow friars had a similar vision, for they are more privy to God's messages than laymen, who live richly on earth, as opposed to spiritual riches. The friar claimed that, among the clergy, only friars remain impoverished and thus are closest to God; and told Thomas that his illness persists because he had given so little to the church.

Thomas claimed that he had indeed given "ful many a pound" to various friars, but never fared the better for it. The friar, characteristically, is irritated that Thomas is not giving all of his money solely to him, and points out to him that a "ferthyng" (a farthing) is not worth anything if split into twelve. Continuing to lecture Thomas, the friar began a long sermon against anger ("ire"), telling the tale of an angry king who sentenced a knight to death , because, as he returned without his partner, the king automatically assumed that the knight had murdered him. When a third knight took the condemned knight to his death, they found the knight that he had supposedly murdered. When they returned to the king to have the sentenced reversed, the king sentenced all three to death: the first because he had originally declared it so, the second because he was the cause of the first's death, and the third because he did not obey the king.

Another ireful king, Cambises, was a drunk. When one of his knights claimed that drunkenness caused people to lose their coordination, Cambyses drew his bow and arrow and shot the knight's son to prove that he still had control of his reflexes. The friar then told of Cyrus, the Persian king who had the river Gyndes destroyed because one of his horses had drowned in it.

At the close of this sermon, the friar asked Thomas for money to build the brothers' cloister. Thomas, annoyed by the friar's hypocrisy, told the friar that he had a gift for him that he was sitting on, but that he would only receive it if he promised to split it up equally between each of the friars.

The friar readily agreed, and put his hand down behind Thomas' back, groping round – and Thomas let out a fart louder than a horse could make. The friar became immediately angry, and promised to repay Thomas for his fart, but, before he could, the servants of the house chased the friar out.

The enraged friar found the lord of the village and told him of the embarrassment he suffered, angrily wondering how he was supposed to divide a fart into twelve. The lord's squire spoke up with a suggestion, in return for a "gowne-clooth" from his master: take a cartwheel, and tell each of twelve friars to lay his nose at the end of a spoke. Then the friar of the tale could sit in the centre of the wheel and fart, and each of the spokes would carry the smell along to the rim – and therefore, divide it up between each of the friars.

Analysis

Chaucer carefully shows us the Summoner, quaking with anger, after hearing the Friar's Tale, and those pious readers who might have thought that the Friar's Tale veered close to the line of blasphemous sin would likely have been straight out offended by the Summoner's. It is a bilious, aggressive tale which does not even consider pulling its punches, and the Friar's contempt is roundly "quyt" with a full-on, unrelenting attack from the Summoner.

Anality is a key ingredient in the tale, potentially a reference to the possible interpretation of the General Prologue which argues that the Summoner and Pardoner are engaged in a homosexual relationship. Regardless of whether this reading is accepted, the prologue begins with a journey into the devil's arse, and the tale finds its resolution with the division of a fart, first from Thomas' arse, and then from the friar's.

This journey from arse to arse is only one of several ways in which the Summoner's Tale mechanically closes in on itself, in precisely the way that the friar within it manages to bring about his own humiliation. There is a neat irony in the way that the friar, after a lengthy lecture about anger management and doing away with "ire" (anger) then becomes absolutely furious, looking as if he were "a wilde boor". The structure of the tale has a "quitting"-like circularity to it.

This circularity also features in individual words: The Summoner's Tale operates on a series of clever puns. At the end of the tale, the division of the fart is a challenge, the lord remarks, in "ars-metrike" – in the art of measurement, but, as Seth Lerer, points out, a challenge too in the metrics of the arse. Moreover, Jankin's vision of the friars gathered at the spokes of a huge wheel is actually a parody of the Pentecost: the day where the twelve apostles receive the Holy Spirit as Christ ascends to heaven. It is, one might suggest, a reworking of religion entirely appropriate to the piety of the friar (and even the Summoner!) in question.

The most significant pun, however, is the most interesting. The friar in the tale berates Thomas, telling him that a "ferthyng" (a farthing coin) is not worth anything split into twelve; and, then, of course, he is paid for the tales he then tells with a farting, which he must split into twelve. The two words were likely homonyms in Middle English, and the punning extends the idea of quitting – which structures this tale and the Friar's as a pair – down into the fabric of the tale itself.

Yet there is another question, which raises a serious point. Is religious advice actually worth people's money? Is the Summoner (or the Friar, or any of the pilgrims) actually telling the company anything which could be valued more highly than a fart? Perhaps Chaucer, aware of the level of potential offense contained within his tale, poses its key question deliberately to those inclined to take it too seriously: isn't tale telling, like farting, just a lot of hot air?

Summary and Analysis of The Clerk's Tale

Prologue to the Clerk's Tale

The Host remarks that the Clerk of Oxford sits as coyly and quietly as a new-married bride, and tells him to be more cheerful: "Telle us som myrie tale!" ("tell us a merry tale"). The Host continues to argue that, when someone is entered into a game, they have to play by the rules of that game; and adds that he doesn't want a tale told in "heigh style", but spoken "pleyn".

The Clerk replies kindly that the Host has the "governance" over the company (is "in charge" of the company) and says that he will tell a tale which he learned from a worthy clerk, Francis Petrarch, who is now dead and nailed into his coffin. He then praises the renowned Petrarch for his sweet rhetoric and poetry; though warns the company, before he begins, that Petrarch wrote a poem in a "high style" exalting the Italian landscape.

The Clerk's Tale

(I)

The tale begins with the description of Saluzzo, a region at the base of Mount Viso in Italy. There was once a marquis of this region named Walter. He was wise, noble and honorable, but his mind was always on seeking immediate pleasures – turning aside more worthy pastime, and even refusing to marry.

The people of his realm confronted him about his steadfast refusal, pleading with him to take a wife, so that his lineage could continue (and so that his son could continue his work in the event of his death). They offer to choose for him the most noble woman in the realm for his wife. He agrees to marry, but makes this one condition: he will marry whomever he chooses, regardless of birth, and his wife shall be treated with the respect accorded to an emperor's daughter, no matter her origin.

He set the day on which he would be married; his people thanked him on their knees, and returned home.

(II)

Not far from the marquis' honorable palace, among the poor people, lived a man named Janicula, who had a daughter Griselde, who was exceedingly virtuous, courageous and charitable. While hunting, the marquis caught sight of Griselde and, recognizing her virtue, immediately decided that this exemplary woman should be his wife.

On the day of the wedding, Walter had not revealed to the public the woman he would marry, and the populace wondered whether he might, in fact, not marry at all. Walter had, however, already prepared rich garments and jewelery in Griselde's size. That morning, the marquis came to Janicula's home and asked him for his permission to marry his daughter. Janicula was so astonished, he turned red, and could not speak – but did manage eventually to assent to the marriage.

Walter, however, wanted Griselde herself to assent before he married her, and, the two men went into her chamber. Walter asked her hand in marriage, and asked her to to be ready to do whatever he said, whenever he said it, but never to resent him; if she agreed to this, he said, he would swear to marry her. Griselde swore never to disobey him – and he took her outside to introduce her to his populace as his new wife.

The marquis' servants took Griselde and dressed her in all new, expensive clothes for the wedding; she appeared as if she had been born as nobility, not from her actual humble origin. Her virtue and excellence became renowned throughout Saluzzo, and in many other regions, for she was essentially a perfect wife – she appeared as "from hevene sent". Soon she gave birth to a baby girl, although she would have preferred a son to be his father's heir.

(III)

Soon after his daughter was born, the marquis decided to test his wife. The narrator, at this stage, explicitly expresses doubt about why the marquis would test his wife: "as for me" he says, I think it sits "yvele" ("evilly") "to assaye a wyf whan that it is no need" ("to test a wife when there is no need to").

The marquis told her that although she was dear to him, to the rest of the nobility she was not. They, he said, objected to her new daughter, and wanted her to be taken away from Griselde and put to death. Griselde received this news without grievance, and answered that she and her child would do anything that pleased her husband. Rather than putting the child to death (though allowing Griselde to believe her child was dead), the marquis instead sent the child away with one of his sergeants to be raised by his sister, the husband of the Earl of Panago, in Bologna. Walter did pity his wife, who remained steadfast and dedicated to him, silently accepting her fate and that of her child whom she believed dead. Griselde never spoke of her daughter, nor even mentioned her name.

(IV)

Four years passed, and Griselde had another child, a boy, and, when it was two years old, Walter repeated the same test. The people, Walter argued, did not want the low blood of Janicula to succeed him as marquis. She accepted this, and told Walter that she realized she was of low birth and would consent to die if it pleased him. However, she did point out that she had had no benefits of motherhood, only the pain of childbirth and a continued pain of losing her children. The same sergeant came to take away her son, and Griselde kissed her child goodbye.

The people came to loathe Walter, thinking that he had murdered his children. Walter, unruffled by their disapproval, devised his next test: organizing the court of Rome to send a counterfeit papal bull which ordered Walter to divorce Griselde and take another wife. Upon hearing this, Griselde remained steadfast.

However, the marquis had written a secret letter to Bologna, ordering the Earl of Panago to return home his children with huge pomp and circumstance, but without telling them whose children they were. Indeed, the Earl was to pretend that the daughter was to marry the marquis himself.

(V)

Walter told Griselde of the papal bull, returned her dowry to her, and sent her back to her father's house. She was stoic upon hearing this, and, though she reiterated her love for Walter, she did not repent for loving him. She only asks that she not be sent naked from the palace, but will be given the simple smock, just the like the ones she used to wear in poverty, to wear to spare her from suffering the indignity of returning home completely unclothed. Walter granted this request, and in, stripping herself of all of her riches, Griselde returned home to her father in her poor clothes once more.

The people followed her home, weeping for her bad fortune, but Griselde herself did not shed a tear, and, as she approached the house, her father ran out to cover her with his old coat. The narrator, at the end of this part, compares the suffering Griselde has endured to that of the biblical Job.

(VI)

The Countess of Panago arrived at Saluzzo from Bologna with Griselde's two children. Walter sent a message to Griselde that he would be married soon and wished for Griselde to plan the ceremony; patiently, Griselde agreed and began to make the arrangements. When the people saw the new wife, they thought, for the first time, seeing her riches and the stately procession, that Walter was right to change his wife.

As the party sat down to dinner, Walter called Griselde into the hall. When he introduced Griselde to his new wife, she pleaded with him not to treat the new wife as unkindly as he did her (not to "prikke with no tormentynge / This tender mayden") but meant no malice in her words.

At that, Walter kissed Griselde and claimed that she had always been his wife. Griselde stood, astonished, like someone who had woken from a sleep. Walter then revealed to her the actual fate of her two children – the supposed new wife was actually Griselde's daughter. Griselde fell down in a swoon, and, on awaking, called her children to her, where she kissed them and held them so tightly that they could not tear the children from her arms. The ladies took her into her chamber, and took her out of her poor clothing, replacing it with a "clooth of gold that brighte shoon", and a coronet on her head. The two lived happily ever after, and, eventually, the son succeeded his father after his father's death, and was kind in marriage.

This story, the Clerk then continues, is not told so that wives should follow Griselde's example in humility - it is impossible that they would. Every person, however, should try to be constant in adversity and in the face of God, like Griselde was to Walter: this is why Petrarch wrote the story. People under God must live in virtuous patience, accepting whatever will God serves on them.

However, the Clerk continues, it were very difficult to find even two or three Griseldes out of a whole town of people nowadays. If you put them to the test, their "gold" has been so mixed in with "brass" that the coin would snap rather than withstand the pressure. For which reason, for the love of the Wife of Bath (whose sect God maintain "in heigh maistrie"), the Clerk continues, I will now sing a song to gladden you.

Lenvoy de Chaucer

Griselde is dead and her patience is too, and both of them are buried in Italy. No wedded man should try his wife's patience in trying to find Griselde: he will fail. The Envoy continues to address "O noble wyves", advising them not to nail down their tongues in humility, or Chichevache will swallow them whole. Follow Echo, that held no silence, and take on the governance yourself, the Envoy continues, and use the arrows of your eloquence to pierce your husband's armor. The conclusion of the Envoy tells fair women to show off their good looks, and ugly women to spend all of their husband's money!

The words of the Host

When the Clerk had finished his tale, the Host swore "By Goddes bones" that he would rather lose a barrel of ale that his wife had – even once – heard this tale. It is a noble tale, he continues – before advising the company not to ask why he'd rather not have his wife hear it.

Analysis

That the Clerk, in a typically clerical touch, gets his tale from a very worthy literary source is not a fiction of Chaucer's. The tale does indeed come from a tale of Petrarch's; yet what the Clerk fails to mention in his citation is that Petrarch himself took it from Bocaccio's *Decameron* (a fact which Chaucer certainly knew). Another thing, surely known to the clerks in Chaucer's audience, that the Clerk omits to mention is that even Petrarch had difficulty interpreting the tale as he found it in Boccaccio. The key problem, in fact, to reading the Clerk's Tale is interpretation.

The tale itself is simple enough: woman of low birth is horribly tested by her noble husband, made to suffer extremely, and eventually, is restored to good fortune. But what does the tale mean? Not, according to the Clerk, at least, what it seems to mean at first reading: that women should patiently submit themselves to their husbands will. This sentiment, of course, is deeply at odds with the Wife of Bath (herself explicitly acknowledged and praised by the Clerk in the tale) and her tale only a little earlier – and the Clerk endorses the Wife's desire for female maistrie.

Yet why is the tale not to be read as endorsing female subjugation to the husband? Perhaps because the Clerk (as he implies) wholeheartedly endorses the maistrie-seeking of the Wife of Bath, but also, as is twice said in the tale, because there are no Griseldes left in the world today. Is this lack of patient Griseldes a sign of progress, or something to be mourned? If the story is a celebration of Griselde's fortitude, the Clerk accurately judges that it would be impossible for any woman to legitimately withstand the suffering that Griselde faced with such resignation; and indeed, her extreme behavior might not even be read as commendable, for she allows her husband to murder her two children without struggle. The Clerk indicates that women should strive toward the example that Griselde sets, but not necessarily follow her example in such an extreme form. Where does one draw the line? The tale could be read as supporting either pro-feminist or anti-feminist sentiments.

Petrarch's solution to the problem is also voiced by the tale: that the tale is not, in fact, about men and women at all, but how men in general should relate to God. This is a perfectly reasonable interpretation, but as presented by Chaucer, Walter – cruel, testing for no obvious reason, and extremely self-satisfied – does not make for a particularly attractive representative of God. Petrarch's interpretation of his own story is not an absolute one: and nor is Chaucer's (it is important to note that the envoy at the very end of the tale is attributed "de Chaucer" and not to the Clerk – perhaps something more significant than a simple print-setting error). For the envoy advises wives not to nail down their tongues, but to attack their husbands and be shrews - a sentiment which the tale does not reflect at all, particularly when you consider that it is Griselde's strength of character and humility which justify her eventual reward and reunion with her children.

Chaucer, Petrarch, and the Wife of Bath – each have separate lines of interpretation for a single tale, and each of them are potentially justified in the text. Yet the Clerk's presentation does not invite the reading of the tale as simply a fable - there is little heightened or distanced in the presentation. In fact, the telling strives to arouse our displeasure at Walter's conduct, and our sympathy for Griselde - Chaucer, in fact, studs the narrative with deeply humanizing, sympathetic details (for example, the way Griselde, reunited with her children, cannot bear to release them from her embrace) which make an allegorical reading of the tale even more difficult. It is difficult to believe that this tale is simply an allegory of man's relationship with God, when the allegory is written with such focused, emotional detail.

One might note too that Griselde is stripped and dressed in new clothes as her status changes from low, to high, back to low, and eventually back to high. The idea of the woman dressed in cloth (cloth, as we noted in the Wife of Bath's tale, is a symbol for text) reflects the unknowability of a woman's heart and mind, as well as the way Griselde herself can be interpreted and reinterpreted (as peasant and as noble wife) in precisely the way that her tale can.

Petrarch is dead and nailed in his coffin, the Clerk emphasizes at the start of the tale – and so is Griselde, he tells us at the end. How either of them felt about the subject matter of the Clerk's Tale is no longer of any relevance; and the complexity and problematic nature of this apparently simply-structured tale depends on just that incitement – how an audience, hearing the tale **now**, interprets and understands it in the context of their own (medieval or modern) attitudes to gender and marriage.

Summary and Analysis of The Merchant's Tale

Prologue to the Merchant's Tale

Following the Clerk's pronouncement on marriage, the merchant claims that he knows all about weeping and wailing as a result of marriage - and so, he thinks, do many people who are married. Even if his wife were to marry the devil, the merchant claims, she would overmatch him. Having been married two months, and having loathed every minute of it, the merchant sees a "long and large difference" between Griselde's patience and his wife's cruelty. The Host asks the merchant to tell a tale of his horrid wife; and, though "for soory herte" (for sorry heart) the merchant claims he cannot tell of his *own* sorrow, he will tell another tale.

The Merchant's Tale

Once there was, dwelling in Lombardy, a worthy knight who had lived nobly for sixty years without a wife. However when this knight, January, had turned sixty, whether out of devotion or dotage, he decided to finally be married. He searched for prospects, now convinced that the married life was a paradise on earth, particularly keen to take a young, beautiful wife.

The narrator then defies Theophrastus, the author of a tract attacking marriage, arguing that a wife is God's gift, which will last longer than any other gift of Fortune. There follows a lengthy passage extolling the virtues of a wife, and the virtue of marriage, citing many biblical examples.

January one day sent for all of his friends, telling them of his intent to marry, explaining that he was ill and old, and wanted a wife no older than twenty, which he could mold like warm wax in his hands. Various men gave him various advice about marriage, some praising it, some arguing against it, and the altercation continued all day. The core of the argument was between Placebo and Justinus. Placebo cited Solomon, advising January that it would be excellent to marry a young wife, and telling him to do exactly as he pleased. Justinus cited Seneca, arguing that January should be more careful and more thoughtful before taking a wife, warning that a young wife was like to cuckold an old husband.

"Straw for thy Senek!" January responds, agreeing with Placebo's response that only a "cursed man" would argue against marriage; and with that word, they all arose and January began to prepare for his wedding. Fair women and fair bodies passed through January's head like images reflected on a mirror set up in a market-place – but eventually, January selected one women from the many available to him.

Calling his friends to him again, January asked them not to make any arguments against what he had resolved to do, and voiced his only concern - that a man who finds perfect happiness on earth, as he would with his wife, would never find a similar happiness in heaven, for one must choose between one perfect happiness and another. Justinus, furious with January's foolishness, advised him that God sent a married man more reason to repent than a single man, and so, married, he might be more likely to get to heaven – even suggesting that marriage might be January's purgatory.

The narrator then, by way of an *occupatio* leaves out the wedding ceremony, but tells us that January married his intended, May, in a lavish and joyous ceremony. Venus, the goddess of love, laughed at all of the guests, as January had become one of her knights: when tender youth has wedded stooping age, the narrator continues, there is such mirth that it cannot be written.

At the end of the feast, the men cast spices around the wedding house, and everyone was full of joy –

except for Damian, the knight's squire, who was so in love with the lady May that he was almost mad. The men rode home, and said their farewells and thanks to January, who then decided he would go to bed. He drank strong spiced and sweetened wines, and many a medical mixture, before taking his fresh wife in his arms, rocking her and kissing her often, his bristly beard scratching her tender skin. January made an apology for the offense he was about to do her, but reminding her that legally, he could do whatever he liked to her body. The two then had sex until the day began to dawn, at which point January awoke, drank some bread in wine, and sang loudly, sitting upright in his bed. Quite what May thought of all this, only God knows, the narrator comments – though she thought his sexual exploits absolutely useless.

However, Damian, had written a love letter to May that he pinned in a silk purse next to his heart. One day, Damian was not attending January, and to cover for him the other squires told January that Damian was sick. May and January sat at dinner, and January decided to send May to visit Damian, to tell him that January would soon visit soon, after he had rested. May went straight to Damian, and, secretly, Damian slipped his letter into her hand: knowing that she could not afford to have it discovered, May hid the letter in her bosom. Reading it later, she tore it up and cast it in the toilet so as not to have it discovered.

May had already decided to return Damian's advances, and replied to his letter telling as much –

taking her letter to his bedroom, putting it under his pillow and giving him a secret handshake. Damian awoke the next morning, his sickness all vanished, and returned to serve January humbly. January's house had a garden so magnificent, the narrator now continues, that even he who wrote Romance of the Rose could not describe its beauty, nor could Priapus accurately describe its art. January loved this garden so much that only he possessed the key to it. In the summer he would go there with May and have sex. January had also, in this time, become blind and became increasingly possessive of his wife, which caused Damian great grief – and May too wept very often, for January was always in her company. However, May and Damian kept in touch via letter, and by various secret signs.

May imprinted January's key to the garden in warm wax, and Damian made a secret copy of the key. The eighth of June came round, and January decided, thanks to the incitement of his wife, to go and have sex in his beautiful garden. He sang a beautiful song to awake his wife and tempt her to the garden, and eventually, January, blind as a stone, and May, unlocked the gate and stepped into the garden.

Damian had already entered the garden, as May had made signs to him to do so, and now she signaled to him to climb up a nearby tree, full of fruit. At this point, the narrator makes an unusual departure from the supposed realism of January's story to narrate the descent of Pluto and Proserpina into the garden, who have a long argument about marriage, citing various classical sources. Pluto, feeling pity for January, wants to restore January's sight so that he can see the villainy about to be done behind his back; Prosperina rejects his argument, telling him that the classical sources which proclaim the evil of women missed out the evil performed by men. Proserpina wants May to have sex with Damian; Pluto wants to restore his sight to prevent it - and Proserpina forcibly ends the argument.

Damian sat high in the pear tree, and May told her husband she longed to pick and eat one of the pears. January bent over so that May could stand on his back to climb the tree - she grabbed a branch, and climbed up into the tree with Damian, who pulled up her dress and began to have sex with her. But, when Pluto saw this, he restored January's sight – and January, seeing his cuckoldry, let out a huge roar and asked his wife what she was doing.

Without missing a beat, May responds that she had been told that the best way to restore January's eyesight was to "struggle" with a man in a tree; January responds that she was not struggling, but having full penetrative sex. In that case, May continues, her medicine is false – January clearly isn't seeing clearly, she argues. And when January asserts that he can see perfectly, May rejoices that she has restored her sight, and persuades January that he did not see her having sex with Damian. January is delighted, kisses her and hugs her, and strokes her on her stomach, leading her home to this house.

Epilogue to the Merchant's Tale

"Goddes mercy!" said the Host, praying God to keep him from such a wife, and noting that clever wives easily deceive foolish men by ducking away from the truth. "I have a wyf", the Host continues, who, though she is poor, is a shrew, always blabbing – and she has several other vices too! The Host then cuts himself off again from discussing his wife, as he worries that someone in the company will report his doing so back to his wife. He is, he claims, clever enough not to reveal everything, and therefore his tale is done.

Analysis

There is a real sense in this tale of goodness slightly gone bad, ripeness becoming slightly rotten. This starts, perhaps, with the opening paean to marriage and the description of January as a worthy, noble knight. It is only as we read on that we realize that, in fact, this apparent positivism is flecked with a bitter irony. January, the noble knight, is also portrayed in unforgiving detail, even down to the scratchy bristles on his neck, and the loose skin on his aged body. We, like May, recoil at the description – there is nothing, for example, of the comfortable, stylized presentation of (for example) the Nun's Priest's Tale here. The narrator is unstinting when he wants to focus our attentions on something unpleasant.

The authorial condemnation of May also departs from the other fabliaux of the Canterbury Tales. Like Alison of the Miller's Tale, she is crafty, but May is also wicked. She escapes without punishment from her husband, but unlike the Miller's Tale this is not a satisfactory conclusion. While the Miller's Tale prized cunning and crafty behavior, the Merchant's Tale adheres to more traditional values. Therefore, May's escape from punishment is a dissonant element of the story, for she behaves contrary to the established values that the Merchant has set for his tale.

May, unlike her husband, largely escapes from the spotlight of the tale – it does not have access to her thoughts (only God knows, at one point, what she thought of her husband) nor does it really describe her body in anything like the detail it lavishes on her husband's. What we see of May is largely a matter of her secret signs and cunning behavior: and the only lengthy description of her, significantly, is given in the context of presenting her as a good option for January to marry. What appears beautiful on the visible outside is clearly rotten in the middle.

This too is represented in the strand of Biblical imagery throughout the tale. It is rather obvious, perhaps, to see May's infidelity with Damien (whose very name, some critics argue, means "snake") as a version of Eve's transgression with the snake – both, indeed, take place in a beautiful garden, though the Bible's Adam does not share the physical disgust of January. Characteristic of the Merchant's apparent bitterness, perhaps, is the remark which follows January's really rather beautiful pastiche (calling May to awake and come into the garden) of the Song of Songs: it refers to them in a blunt, dismissive phrase as "olde, lewed words". In this tale, beautiful women are really venomous, malicious tricksters - beautiful, lyrical poetry is really only old, obscene words.

May, however, despite her low blood, proves herself hugely more intelligent than her noble husband: we might also find analogues for this (at least in sympathy, if not in intelligence) in Griselde of the Clerk's Tale. There is nothing of the indulgent, joyful trickery of the Miller's Tale in the Merchant's Tale, but instead a return to the signification of the Reeve's Tale - the moment of sexual intercourse is presented with the same unflinching, uneuphemistic detail, and the preceding action between the illicit lovers in both tales is largely a matter of signs.

Secret signs are everywhere in the Merchant's Tale: things which, like the mirror in the common marketplace (the metaphor for January's pre-wedding fanciful mind), leave a certain impression on the mind. From the letter that May reads and then casts into the privy, to the secret handshake between May and Damien, to the impression of January's key which allows Damien into the garden, this tale is focused on tricky actions rather than words, secret, illicit events rather than open actions.

The bitterness of the Merchant, trapped in his unhappy marriage, can be felt, then, coursing through the veins of the Merchant's Tale at various points; but particularly in its bitterly unhappy (happy) ending, in which blind January is entirely gulled into believing that he has not been made a fool of. Moreover, when we consider that January happily strokes his wife on her "wombe" ("stomach", but also "womb") at the end of the tale, the Merchant might even leave us with a taste of what would happen next: has May just become pregnant with Damien's baby? The suggestion is not as ridiculous as it initially sounds - particularly when you consider that the pear (it is a pear tree in which the couple have sex) was a well-known remedy to help fertility in Chaucer's day. Perhaps May – at the end of this tale – has actually got something (someone!) rotten growing inside her.

Summary and Analysis of The Squire's Tale

Introduction to the Squire's Tale

The Host asks the Squire to draw near and tell the next tale.

The Squire's Tale

(I)

The Squire tells the tale of Cambyuskan, the king of Sarai in Tartary. With his wife Elpheta he had two sons, Algarsyf and Cambalo, and a daughter Canacee (previously mentioned by the Man of Law). In the twentieth year of his reign, on the Ides of March, his subjects celebrated his nativity. During the great feast with the king and his knights, a strange knight came into the hall on a brass horse, carrying a broad mirror of glass, wearing a gold ring on his thumb and carrying a naked sword by his side.

This knight saluted the king and queen, and all the lords, in order, so reverently and nobly that even Gawain could not have bettered him. The narrator apologizes for not being able to reproduce the nobility of his elocution, punning that he could not climb "over so heigh a style", and resolving only to reproduce the meaning, not the expression, of what the knight said.

This knight had been sent from the king of Arabia and India, to bring Cambyuskan a steed of brass that could, within twenty-four hours, transport a person safely anywhere on the globe. He also presented to Canacee a mirror that foresaw impending mischance and could determine the character of friends and foes, and a ring that enabled the wearer to understand the language of any bird, and the healing properties of all herbs. His final gift was the sword, whose edge would bite through any armor but whose flat would cure any wounds inflicted by the edge.

Having told his tale, the knight rode out of the hall, leaving his steed standing in the court, and was led to his chamber. The presents were carried into the tower, and the ring given to Canacee, but the brass steed would not move until the knight taught people how to move it. The horse was a source of wonder for the people, compared alternately to the Pegasus and the Trojan horse. All one had to do to move the brass horse was to twirl a peg in its ear, according to the knight.

(II)

After the revelry of the night before, the next morning everybody but Canacee remained asleep until late. She had dreamt of the mirror and the ring and thus had her first satisfying rest in a very long time. As she went out walking that morning with her maids, she came across a bleeding peregrine falcon that cried out in anguish. It had maimed itself. Canacee picked up the falcon and spoke to it, a power she had gained from the ring the knight had given her. The falcon told her a tale of a handsome tercelet as treasonous and false as he was beautiful, who fell in love with a kite as well as with the falcon, and left the falcon to love the kite. Canacee healed the bird with herbs which she dug out of the ground, and carried it to a box, covered in blue velvets, with a painted meadow inside it, which she laid by her bedside.

The narrator then leaves Canace, promising to return to the story of her ring and show how the falcon regained her love, thanks to the mediation of Cambalo, the king's son. First, the narrator says, he will tell of Cambyuskan, and how he won his cities, and after that of Algarsyf, and how he won his wife (for whom he would have been in great peril, were it not for the brass horse) and after that of Cambalo, who fought with the brothers in order to win Canacee, and then – after all that – the narrator intends to pick up where he left off.

(III)

The narrator has just begun to set the scene, when he is interrupted…

The words of the Franklin to the Squire and the words of the Host to the Franklin

The Franklin tells the Squire that he has served himself well, praising his wit, and asserting that no-one in the company is as eloquent as the Squire. The Franklin then comments that he would give twenty pounds worth of land if his own son were a man of such discretion as the Squire – who needs possessions, if he is virtuous! The Franklin continues that he has often rebuked his own son for not listening to virtuous people - the Franklin's son only plays at dice and spends money, and would rather talk with a page than a nobleman.

At this point, the Host interrupts - "Straw for youre gentillesse!" ("Straw to your nobility!") – reminding the Franklin that what he is saying is irrelevant, and that each pilgrim must tell at least a tale or two, or break his vow. The Franklin reassures the Host that he is aware of this, even if he is taking a moment to speak to the Squire, and – as instructed by the host – tells his tale, commenting that, if it pleases the Host, his tale will certainly be a good one.

Analysis

Since the Squire's Tale exists only in a fragmentary form, it is difficult to determine precisely how we are supposed to read it. The tale may be a fragment because Chaucer never finished the tale or because the later section of the tale was lost in the manuscripts from which the Canterbury Tales were taken. And yet, the Franklin's interruption comes at a point which suggests that the Squire's Tale might be one of Chaucer's many trick interrupted-endings (see, for example, his *House of Fame*, or

Chaucer's Tale of Sir Thopas).

For the moment at which the Franklin interrupts comes only two lines after the Squire has outlined his plans – extremely lengthy plans – for the rest of his tale, giving as the last plot point to be covered in his telling Cambalo's fight for the hand of Canacee. There seems nothing very unusual about that, until we remember that, at the start of the tale, we are clearly told that Canacee and Cambalo are brother and sister. And this is where the tale becomes interesting. Canacee, of course, is the person discussed in the Man of Law's Prologue - Chaucer, the Man of Law claims, will not tell her story, and nor will he.

Yet here is Chaucer, in the mouth of the Squire, promising to tell the story of incestuous Canacee. It is certainly true that the Squire's plan for the rest of his tale looks as if it might take four pilgrimages of its own to complete – the Squire, the son of the Knight, certainly inherited his father's long-windedness – and some critics have argued that the Franklin breaks off the tale (either with irony or with faux modesty and compliments) only to prevent the pilgrimage from having to endure all of it. Yet critics – who have paid scant attention to the Squire's Tale, often disregarding it as unfinished – have yet to come up with a fully persuasive explanation of why it is the promise of incest which seems to motivate the abrupt termination of the Squire's Tale.

William Kamowski has also pointed out that the abridgement of the Squire's Tale precedes an abridgement of the Host's original tale-telling plan:

> In fact, at the very moment when the Squire breaks off, an apparent reshaping of the grand plan for the Canterbury Tales also takes place. Harry Bailly reminds the Franklin, "wel thou woost / That ech of yow moot tellen atte leste / A tale or two, or breken his biheste" (696-98). Evidently the Host's original plan for four tales apiece will not be realized. It seems more than coincidence that the Host trims his own colossal ambition so soon after the aborting of the Squire's grand plan, which is too large to be realized within the framework of either the Host's storytelling contest or Chaucer's frame narrative.

There are lots of interesting avenues for exploration and interpretation with the Squire's Tale, yet it only seems fair to conclude that the critical work on the Tale remains, like the Tale itself, frustratingly inconclusive.

Summary and Analysis of The Franklin's Tale

Prologue to the Franklin's Tale

The old Bretons, in their time, made songs, and the Franklin's Tale, the narrator says, is to be one of those songs. However, the Franklin begs the indulgence of the company because he is a "burel man" (an unlearned man) and simple in his speech. He has, he says, never learned rhetoric, and he speaks simply and plainly – the colors he knows are not colors of rhetoric, but colors of the meadow.

The Franklin's Tale

The Franklin's Tale begins with the courtship of the Breton knight Arviragus and Dorigen, who came to be married happily. Their marriage was one of equality, in which neither of the two was master or servant; and the narrator comments specifically that when "maistrie" (the desire of the Wife of Bath and the women in her tale) enters into a marriage, love flaps its wings and flies away.

However, soon after their marriage, Arviragus was sent away to Britain to work for two years. Dorigen wept for his absence, despite the letters that he sent home to her. Her friends would often take her on walks where they would pass the cliffs overlooking the ocean and watch ships enter the port, hoping that one of them would bring home her husband. However, although her friends' comforting eventually started to work, Dorigen remained distressed by the grisly, black rocks visible from the cliff-side, near to the shore. She asked God why he would create "this werk unresonable" (this unreasonable work), whose only purpose was to kill people. Her friends, seeing how terribly Dorigen feared that whatever ship brought her husband home would crash on these rocks and sink, provided further distractions.

One day, her friends had organized a party and a dance in a beautiful garden. It was at this dance that Aurelius, a squire, danced in front of Dorigen, who was as fresh and well-dressed as the month of May. His singing and dancing were better than any man's, and he was one of the most handsome men alive. Unbeknownst to Dorigen, Aurelius had been in love with her for two years, but had never dared tell her how he felt. It was during the dancing, then, that Aurelius addressed Dorigen, wishing that he, and not her husband, had been sent across the sea, before begging her to have mercy on him and revealing his love.

Dorigen responded by sternly rebuking Aurelius, telling him that she would never be an untrue wife, and had no intention of cuckolding her husband. And then, "in pley" (playfully, flirtily, in fun), Dorigen added that she would be Aurelius' love on the day that all of the rocks were removed from the coast. This made Aurelius sigh heavily: "Madame", he said "this were an inpossible!" (an impossibility). The dance ended and the guests went home, except for poor, sorrowful Aurelius, who fell to his knees, and holding his hands to heaven, prayed to the gods for mercy.

Arviragus then returned from abroad, and Dorigen was delighted to have him back. Two years passed, and Aurelius lay in torment, and without comfort – except, that is for his brother, a clerk, who suggested that he meet a student of law at Orleans who was versed in the sciences of illusion and "magyk". Heading toward Orleans, the two came across a young clerk, roaming by himself, who greeted them in Latin, and claimed to know why they came. And before they went a step further, he told them exactly what they were travelling to achieve.

Aurelius leapt down from his horse, and went with this man to his house, where he fed them and showed them wondrous illusions of various kinds. The man eventually agreed to remove the rocks from the coast for a thousand pounds; "Fy on a thousand pound!" responded Aurelius, "This wyde world... I wolde it yeve" ("Never mind a thousand pounds! I'd give you the wide world!"), and promised to pay the man.

The next morning, having stayed at the man's house, they travelled to Brittany, where, by illusion, the man made it so that, for a week or two, it would appear that the rocks had vanished. Aurelius, who now knew that there was no obstacle to his deal with Dorigen, said grateful prayers, and eventually came to his lady and explained to her, in courtly, formal terms, how he had fulfilled their bargain. She stood astonished, entirely white, never thinking that such an occasion could arise, and went home, despairing.

Arvigarus was out of town, and Dorigen was overcome with grief, realizing that she must forfeit either her body or her reputation. She thought about the numerous instances in which a faithful wife or a maiden destroyed herself rather than submitting herself to another. She cited the maidens of Lacedaemon who chose to be slain rather than defiled, Hasdrubal's wife, who committed suicide during the siege of Carthage, and Lucrece, who did the same when Tarquin took her by force.

When Arviragus returned home and Dorigen told him the truth of what had happened, he told that he will bear the shame of her actions, and that adhering to her promise is the most important thing. He therefore sent her to submit to Aurelius. When Aurelius learned how well Arviragus had accepted his wife's promise, Aurelius decided to let Dorigen's promise go unfulfilled, refusing to break the married couple's "trouthe". He claimed that a squire can indeed be as honorable as a knight. Aurelius then went to pay the law student, even though his affair remained unconsummated, and the man forgave Aurelius' debt, proving *himself* honorable. The narrator ends the tale by posing the question to the assembled company "Which was the mooste fre, as thynketh yow?" ("Who was the most generous/noble, do you think?").

Analysis

The Franklin's Tale is, as the narrator acknowledges at the start, a *Breton lay*, a brief romance supposedly descending from Celtic origins, and usually dealing with themes of romance, love and usually containing some sort of supernatural ingredient. Chaucer took the story from Boccaccio's *Decameron* though the tale weaves well into many of the other Tales, including the Merchant's Tale, which is echoed in many of the Franklin's descriptions.

The tale seems to offer the solution to the problem raised and complicated in the other "Marriage Group" tales in its initial comments that "maistrie" has no place in love. Dorigen and Arvigarus are among the few happy couples in Chaucer's Tales, and yet one suspects that the problem of "maistrie" is sidelined so as to focus on an entirely different problem, and one close to the heart of the Tales: the problem of language, words, and keeping one's word.

"Trouthe" is a central word in the tale, meaning "fidelity", and "truth", as well as "keeping one's word", and the idea of pledging troth (an Elizabethanism) – giving one's word as a binding promise – is central to the agreements between Dorigen and Aurelius. What the Franklin's Tale shows us is not dissimilar from the Friar's Tale - that we have to watch what we say because, like Dorigen's promise made "in pley", we never quite know how things are going to work out. The word becomes the marker of the deed, and, not to break her word, Dorigen is almost forced to perform the deed. In a work so concerned with stories and tale-telling, it is significant that Chaucer (as in the Friar's and Manciple's Tales) takes time to remind us of the value of each individual word we speak, and write.

The tale itself, of course, also bequeaths a word to both of its audiences (that is, the pilgrim audience of characters and the real-world audience reading or listening to Chaucer) and asks us to evaluate it in relation to what we have heard. "Fre", the root of our modern word "free", can mean generous (i.e. to give freely) but also has overtones of nobleness, "good behavior". Who, then, is the most generous and noble at the end of the tale?

Arviragus, Jill Mann argues, by being noble enough to become a cuckold to preserve his wife's reputation, sparks off a chain of passivity, which she thinks is an extremely positive thing. Arviragus giving up his rights in Dorigen leads to Aurelius giving up his which in turn leads to the law student giving up his. When one person backs down, Mann interprets, so will the rest of the world.

Mann's is an interesting reading, but it does not quash entirely the thought that Arviragus' priorities might be in the wrong order - is it really more important that his wife holds to a bargain (made only in jest) rather than she sleeps with someone she does not want to sleep with?

Or at least, so she says. It is worth noting that, on Aurelius' first appearance, the tale stresses his good looks and charm, and one wonders precisely what motivates Dorigen, even in jest (and Freud has much to say about the meaning of jokes) to make the bargain. For surely Dorigen is the person who, were the bargain to go ahead, gets the best deal - not only is her husband safely home (and the rocks, for the moment, vanished) but she gets to sleep with both (extremely handsome, so the tale says) men. How, in fact, has Dorigen been generous or free at all?

Is Aurelius perhaps the most generous: willingly giving up the thing he most desired? Perhaps – but we might perhaps also argue that the thing he gave up, he had no real right to have anyway, considering that the "thing" was sex with another man's wife. The same might be said of the law student, who foregoes only money: a lot of money, but still only money. The question of nobility and generousness completely depends from which perspective you read the tale.

Interestingly, we are never told that Dorigen goes to check whether the rocks have in fact vanished or not. Of course, they only exist as a plot twist within a tale – though one of the things the tale's final question reminds us of is that an existence in words, like the rash promise that Dorigen made, is an existence we dismiss at our peril.

Summary and Analysis of The Physician's Tale

The Physician's Tale

As Titus Livius tells us, there was once a knight called Virginius who had many friends, much wealth, and a loving wife and daughter. The daughter possessed a beauty so great that even Pygmalion could not have created her equal. She was also humble in speech and avoided events which might compromise her virtue. The narrator then breaks off to address governesses and parents, telling them to bring up their children to be virtuous.

The maid one day went into the town, toward a temple, with her mother, where a judge who governed the town, saw the knight's daughter, and lusted after her. He was so caught by the maid's beauty that he concluded "This mayde shal be myn". At that, the devil ran into his heart, and taught him how he, by trickery, could have the maid for his own. He sent after a churl, who he knew was clever and brave, and told him the plan, giving him precious, expensive gifts for his complicity.

The judge's name was Appius, the narrator now tells us, before asserting "So was his name, for this is no fable", but a "historial thyng notable" (a notable historical event). The false churl, Claudius, made a complaint against Virginius, and the judge summoned him to hear the charge against him. Claudius, in short, claimed that Virginius was holding one of his servants, a beautiful young girl, against his will, and pretending she was his daughter. The judge did not listen to Virginius' argument in his own defense, but ordered that the girl be taken as a ward of the court.

Virginius returned home, and called his daughter, with an ashen face. He explained to her that now there were only two avenues open to her: either death or shame. Virginius decided, in a long, mournful speech to his daughter, to kill her, and, although she begged for mercy and another solution, eventually she asked for a little leisure to contemplate her death. She then fell into a swoon, and when she awoke, she blessed God that she could die a virgin. Virginius then took his sword and cut off her head, and took it to the judge.

When the judge saw the head, he tried to escape and hang himself, but soon a thousand people thrust in, knowing of the false iniquity, took Appius and threw him into prison. Claudius was sentenced to be hanged upon a tree – except that Virginius pleaded on his behalf, succeeding in reducing the sentence to exile.

Here, the narrator says, may men see that sin has no reward – even if it is so private that no-one knows of it other than God and the sinner. The last counsel the tale presents us with: "Forsaketh synne, er synne yow forsake" (abandon sin, before sin abandons [destroys] you).

Analysis

After the Physician's Tale has finished, in the prologue to the Pardoner's Tale, the Host claims that he has almost "caught a cardynacle" – almost had a heart attack, and it is not difficult to see why. This is a tale which takes no prisoners: with no prologue to ease us in, this brutal, harsh, violent and uncompromising tale refuses to be read as a fable ("this is no fable") or allegory, but insists that we view its cruel and unpleasant events as things which happen in the real world. One rather wonders why the Physician thinks it will win him the prize at the end of the tale-telling.

Moreover, the tale rushes towards its unpleasant conclusion, even at the expense of plausibility. Why doesn't Virginius try to argue with the judge, or call upon the mob of thousand people who, only a little later, burst through the doors to deliver justice? Why doesn't Virginius hide his daughter, or jump on his knightly steed and escape to another land? Again, as in the Knight's Tale and the Franklin's Tale, there seems to be some interrogation of ideas of chivalry: this is a man who, without any need for reflection, would rather preserve his daughter's nobility and honor than keep her alive. Chaucer again casts a negative light across the codes of honor to which men adhere.

Critics have not devoted much attention to the tale, except to say that it provides, perhaps, the first significant "death's head" in the Canterbury Tales: what hitherto has been a fun, "game"-some party, a well-meaning competition, despite its squabbles, is suddenly presented with a tale entirely without good-naturedness or comedy. It is the beginning of a turn toward darkness which entirely changes the tone and tenor of the Tales as a whole, and – although in its criticism of hypocrisy, defense of religion and beauty, and painful, final justice, it has much in common thematically with some of the other tales – it is a tale which seems decidedly set apart from its predecessors.

Summary and Analysis of The Pardoner's Tale

The Introduction to the Pardoner's Tale

Following the Physician's Tale, the Host began to swear as if he were mad, wishing a shameful death on the judge and his advocates, and concluding that the cause of the maiden's death was her "beautee". The Host pronounced the tale a piteous one to listen to, and prayed to God that he protect the Physician's body.

The Host, concluding that he has almost "caught a cardynacle" (had a heart attack) after the brutality of the Physician's Tale, decides that he must have medicine in the form of a merry tale, in order to restore his heart. Turning to the Pardoner, he asks for some "myrthe or japes right anon", and the Pardoner agrees, though, before he begins, he stops at an alehouse to "drynke and eten of a cake". The company protests that the Pardoner not be allowed to tell them a ribald tale, but insists instead on "som moral thyng" - a request which the Pardoner also grants.

The Pardoner's Prologue

Radix malorum est Cupiditas (Greed is the root of all evil)

The Pardoner begins by addressing the company, explaining to them that, when he preaches in churches, his voice booms out impressively like a bell, and his theme is always that greed is the root of all evil. First, the Pardoner says, he explains where has come from, and shows his papal bulls, indulgences, and glass cases crammed full of rags and bones, which he claims (to the congregation, at least) are holy relics with magical properties.

Then, the Pardoner invites anyone who has sinned to come and offer money to his relics, and therefore to be absolved by the Pardoner's power. This trick, the Pardoner says, has earned him at least a hundred marks since he was made a pardoner - and when the "lewd peple" are seated, he continues to tell them false trickeries and lies. His intention, he says, is simply "for to wynne" (to profit), and "nothyng for correccioun of synne" (and nothing to do with the correction of sin); the Pardoner doesn't care whether, after burial, his congregation's souls go blackberry picking. Thus, the Pardoner says, he spits out his venom under the pretense of holiness, seeming holy, pious, and "trewe". "Greed is the root of all evils", the Pardoner quotes again, explaining that he preaches against the same vice which he himself is guilty of. Yet, although he knows he is guilty of the sin, he can still make other people turn away from it.

Next, the Pardoner tells the company how he tells his congregation "olde stories" from long ago, "for lewed peple loven tales olde". He will not, he says, work with hands and make baskets, but get money, wool, cheese and wheat for himself, even if it is from the poorest page or poorest widow in a village. He will drink "licour of the vyne", and have a "joly wenche" in every town. "Now hold your pees!" he shouts to the company, and begins his tale.

The Pardoner's Tale

There once lived in Flanders a company of three rioters who did nothing but engage in irresponsible and sinful behavior. At this point, the narrator interrupts the tale itself to launch a lengthy diatribe against drunkenness - mentioning Herod, Seneca, Adam, Sampson, Attila the Hun and St. Paul as either sources or famed drunkards. This in turn oddly becomes a diatribe against people whose stomachs are their gods (their end, we are told, is death), and then a diatribe against the stomach, called, at one point a "stynkyng cod, fulfilled of dong and of corrupcioun" (a stinking bag, full of dung and decayed matter). This distraction from the story itself ends with an attack on dice-playing (dice here called "bicched bones", or cursed dice).

The three drunkards were in a tavern one night, and, hearing a bell ring, looked outside to see men carrying a corpse to its grave. One of them called to his slave to go and ask who the corpse was: he was told by a boy that the corpse was an old fellow whose heart was smashed in two by a secret thief called Death. This drunkard agreed, and discussed with his companions how this "Death" had indeed slain many people, of all ranks, of both sexes, that very year. The three then made a vow (by "Goddes digne bones") to find Death and slay him.

When they had gone not even half a mile, they met an old, poor man at a style, who greeted them courteously. The proudest of the drunkards responded rudely, asking the man why he was still alive at such a ripe age. The old man answered that he was alive, because he could not find anyone who would exchange their youth for his age - and, although he knocked on the ground, begging it to let him in, he still did not die. Moreover, the old man added, it was not courteous of the drunkards to speak so rudely to an old man.

One of the other drunkards responded still more rudely that the old man was to tell them where Death was, or regret not telling them dearly. The old man, still polite, told the drunkards they could find Death up the crooked way and underneath an oak tree.

The drunkards ran until they came to the tree, and, underneath it, they found eight bushels of gold coins. The worst one of them spoke first, arguing that Fortune had given them the treasure to live their life in happiness - but realizing that they could not carry the gold home without people seeing them and thinking them thieves. Therefore, he suggested, they should draw lots, and one of them should run back to the town to fetch bread and wine, while the other two protected the treasure. Then, at night, they could agree where to take the treasure and carry it safety. This was agreed, and lots were drawn: the youngest of them was picked to go to the town.

However, as soon as he had gone to the town, the two remaining drunkards plotted amongst themselves to stab him upon his return, and then split the gold between them. While he was in the town, the youngest thought of the beauty of the gold coins, and decided to buy some poison in order to kill the other two, keeping the gold for himself. Thus, he went to an apothecary, bought some "strong and violent" poison, poured it into two of three wine bottles (the third was for him to drink from), topped them up with wine, and returned to his fellows.

Exactly as the other two had planned it, it befell. They killed him on his return, and sat down to enjoy the wine before burying his body – and, as it happened, drank the poison and died. The tale ends with a short sermon against sin, asking God to forgive the trespass of good men, and warning them against the sin of avarice, before (this, we can presume narrated in the Pardoner's voice) inviting the congregation to "come up" and offer their wool in return for pardons.

The tale finished, the Pardoner suddenly remembers that he has forgotten one thing - that he is carrying relics and pardons in his "male" (pouch, bag) and begins to invite the pilgrims forward to receive pardon, inciting the Host to be the first to receive his pardon. "Unbokele anon thy purs", he says to the Host, who responds that the Pardoner is trying to make him kiss "thyn old breech" (your old pants), swearing it is a relic, when actually it is just painted with his shit. I wish, the Host says, I had your "coillons" (testicles) in my hand, to shrine them in a hog's turd.

The Pardoner is so angry with this response, he cannot speak a word, and, just in time, the Knight steps in, bringing the Pardoner and the Host together and making them again friends. This done, the company continues on its way.

Analysis

The Pardoner has – in recent years – become one of the most critically discussed of the Canterbury pilgrims. His tale is in many ways the exemplar of the contradiction which the structure of the Tales themselves can so easily exploit, and a good touchstone for highlighting precisely how Chaucer can complicate an issue without ever giving his own opinion.

Thus the Pardoner embodies precisely the textual conundrum of the Tales themselves - he utters words which have absolutely no correlation with his actions. His voice, in other words, is entirely at odds with his behavior. The Pardoner's voice, at the beginning of his tale, rings out "as round as gooth a belle", summoning his congregation: and yet his church is one of extreme bad faith. There is a genuine issue here about whether the Pardoner's tale, being told by the Pardoner, can actually be the "moral" (325) tale it claims to be. For, while the tale does indeed demonstrate that money is the root of all evil, does it still count when he is preaching "agayn that same vice / Which that I use, and that is avarice" (against the very vice I commit: avarice")? How far, in other words, can the teller negate his own moral?

Yet the real problem is that the Pardoner is a successful preacher, and his profits point to several people who do learn from his speeches and repent their sin. His Tale too is an accurate demonstration of the way greed and avarice lead to evil. Hollow execution nevertheless, the Pardoner is an excellent preacher against greed. His voice, in short, operates regardless of his actions. Hollow sentiments produce real results.

This is also reflected in the imagery of the tale itself. The Pardoner hates full stomachs, preferring empty vessels, and, though his "wallet" may well be "bretful of pardoun comen from Rome" (687) but the moral worth of this paper is nil: the wallet, therefore, is full and empty at the same time – exactly like the Pardoner's sermon.

In just the same way Chaucer himself in the Tales can ventriloquize the sentiments of the pilgrim – the Reeve, the Pardoner, the Merchant – and so on, without actually committing to it. Because the Tales themselves, in supposedly reproducing the "telling" of a certain pilgrim, actually do enact precisely the disembodied voice which the Pardoner represents. The moral paradox of the Pardoner himself is precisely the paradox of the Tales and their series of Chaucer-ventriloquized disembodied voices.

There is a doubleness, a shifting evasiveness, about the Pardoner's double audience: the imaginary congregation he describes, and the assembled company to whom he preaches, and tells his "lewed tales", even calling them forth to pardon at the end. The point is clear: even though they know it is insincere, the Pardoner's shtick might still work on the assembled company.

The imagery of the Pardoner's Tale also reflects this fundamental hollowness. The tale itself is strewn with bones, whether in the oath sworn "by Goddes digne bones", whether in the word for cursed dice ("bones") or whether in the bones which the Pardoner stuffs into his glass cases, pretending they are relics. The literary landscape is strewn with body parts, and missing, absent bodies: beginning with the anonymous corpse carried past at the beginning of his tale. Bones, stomachs, coillons – words for body parts cover the page, almost as a grim reminder of the omnipresence of death in this tale.

The General Prologue, suggesting that the Pardoner resembles a "gelding or a mare", hints that the Pardoner may be a congenital eunuch or, taken less literally, a homosexual, and, as the Host seems to suggest at the end, might well be without his "coillons", a Middle English word meaning both "relics" and "testicles". All of the "relics" in this Tale, including the Pardoner's, evade the grasp of the hand. The Pardoner thus can be categorized along with the other bizarrely feminized males in the Tales, including Absolon, Sir Thopas, and, if we believe the Host, Chaucer (the character).

And of course, at the center of the tale, there is a search for somebody called "Death" which, naturally, does not find the person "Death", but death itself. It is a successful – but ultimately unsuccessful – search. All that is left over at the center of the Tales is the bushels of gold, sitting under a tree unclaimed. The root of the tale, as its moral similarly suggests about the root of evil, is money: and money was, to a medieval reader, known to be a spiritual "death". Notably, moreover, in the tale, both "gold" and "death" shift from metaphor to reality and back again; a neat reminder of the ability of the Tales to evade our grasp, raising difficult questions without ever answering them.

Summary and Analysis of The Shipman's Tale

The Shipman's Tale

A rich merchant, who lived at St. Denis, foolishly took a beautiful woman for his wife. She drained his income by demanding clothes and other fine array to make her appear even more beautiful. There was also a fair, bold young monk, perhaps only thirty years old, who was always at the merchant's house. Indeed, he was as welcome there as it is possible for any friend to be. The monk was generous with his money, and always brought gifts for his lord and for the servants, according to their degree.

One day, as he was going to make a journey to Bruges, the merchant invited John to visit him and his wife before he departed. The monk and the merchant had a merry time together, eating and drinking for two days. On the third day, on which the merchant was ready to depart for Bruges, he awoke early and went to his counting-house to balance his books. John was also awake early and went into the garden to pray. The wife went into the garden, worried that something was bothering the monk. He in turn worries about her; he thinks that she did not sleep well, for the merchant kept her up all night having sex – and she admits, in turn, that in fact she has no lust for her husband. John realizes that there is more to this, and promises to keep everything she tells him secret.

The wife complains that her husband is the "worste man that ever was sith that the world bigan" (the worst man ever to have existed since the world began"). She also tells him that she owes a debt of one hundred franks, which, if she does not pay (and her husband finds out about it) will disgrace her. The wife begs the monk to lend her the money.

The noble monk tells the wife that he pities her, and promises to "deliver" the wife "out of this care", and bring her one hundred franks. With that, he caught her by the thighs, embraced her hard, and kissed her many times. The two then parted, and the wife went to her husband in his counting-house, begging him to leave his accounts. The merchant refused, explaining to her that it was essential that he managed his business carefully, as many merchants went bankrupt.

The three dined together that evenings, and after dinner, the monk took the merchant to one side, and asked him to lend him one hundred franks – and the merchant humbly and generously agreed, telling him to pay it again when he could afford to. He fetched the sum and took it to the monk, and no-one in the world but the two of them knew of the loan. That evening, the monk returned to the abbey, and, the next morning, the merchant travelled to Bruges to conduct his business.

The next Sunday, the monk returned to St. Denis, with head and beard all clean and freshly shaved, and – to get to the point – the wife agreed with the monk that, in exchange for the hundred franks, the monk could have sex with the wife all night, a promise which the two of them eagerly fulfilled. The next morning, the monk rode home to his abbey, or wherever pleased him.

The merchant returned home, and, delighted to see his wife, told her about his business transactions - and, when he came into town, he went straight to see his friend, the monk. The monk was delighted to see him, and, after talking about his business trip, the monk told the merchant that he had left his thousand franks with his wife. The merchant went home happy, and his wife met him at the gates – and the two of them had a happy night in bed, until the wife waylaid him, teasing him wantonly. Finally, the merchant told her he was a little angry with her because she had not told him she had received his money from the monk.

However, the wife was not frightened or taken aback by this, but said quickly and boldly that she had indeed received gold from the monk. The wife then argued that she should be allowed to keep the gold, to pay for good hospitality and to do with as she pleased; and, in return for him giving her his money, she would give him her body: "I wol nat paye yow but abedde". And the merchant saw that there was no other option but to agree.

The merry words of the Host to the Shipman and to the lady Prioress

"Wel seyd", the Host compliments the Shipman, cursing the monk, and warning the men in the company to beware of similar tricks. The monk, the Host interprets, tricked both the man and his wife. Moving forward, the Host then looks for the next tale-teller, and courteously asks the Prioress whether she might tell the next tale: "Gladly", she assents, and begins her tale.

Analysis

Despite its relative brevity, the Shipman's Tale interrogates and complicates several key issues raised in earlier tales. After the darker reaches of the Physician's and Pardoner's Tales, the Shipman's Tale returns to fabliau origins, presenting a reasonably simple "trick" story, complicated by Chaucer in the telling.

Primarily, the tale continues the idea, previously raised in The Wife of Bath's tale, that money, sex, and women are closely inter-connected. It is interesting that, in the second fragment, the Shipman promises to tell his tale, mentioning his "joly body" (attractive figure). Scholars have argued that, in fact, the lines about the Shipman's "joly body" were intended to be adapted into the mouth of the Wife of Bath, and it is the Wife of Bath's Tale which immediately follows the Shipman's promise. The bawdy fabliau of the Shipman's Tale is usually assumed to have been intended to be The Wife of Bath's tale before the version we currently have was composed.

Moreover, the Shipman's would not be an unlikely tale for the Wife to have told. At the end, when the Host concludes that the monk tricked both the merchant and his wife, he seems not to have realized the victor at the very end of the tale. Rather like in the Miller's and the Franklin's Tales, we are asked to consider each of the participants at the very close of the tale, and decide who we think has come off best. It is clearly not the merchant, though he has made huge profits in his business dealings, and had his loan repaid, and, though (as the Host argues) the monk has had sex with the wife, remained friends with the merchant, and got off scot-free, it is the wife herself who seems to triumph. Not only has she had enjoyable sex with both the merchant *and* the monk, but she is one hundred franks better off; and she coerces her husband into agreeing to "pay" in return for sleeping with her.

Like the Wife of Bath, this wife has realized the inherent value of her sexual attractiveness: and in a way that seems to a modern reader uncomfortably close to prostitution, she bears out the Wife's dictum that the "bele chose" is in fact an excellent bargaining tool for women to get what they want from men. As the Man of Law's Tale suggested, the female is a pawn in business transactions, and yet, what the Wives (of bath, and of the merchant in this tale) realize that Constance never even considers, is their own potential profitability. If women's bodies are valuable, these two women seem to say, then why shouldn't we be the ones to profit from our bodies?

One also notices the importance attached in these business dealings to giving one's word, to agreements sealed with kisses and with handshakes, and of one thing being verbally exchanged for another before the words become actions – a reminder, perhaps, of the issues of contracts raised by the Franklin's Tale.

Chaucer ties up these concerns, as so often, in a single pun: "taillynge", which means "credit" (and which the narrator wishes upon the company at the end of the tale) is a close relation to "telling" (i.e. telling a tale) but also punningly relates to "tail", Middle English slang for the female genitals. A woman's "tail" becomes an endless credit note: she will pay her husband, she says, in bed. Women, in this tale, and in the Wife of Bath's are playing by patriarchal rules in order to beat the men; and the fact that they do beat the men might have been an uncomfortable shift of powers to many of Chaucer's medieval readers.

Summary and Analysis of The Prioress' Tale

Prologue of the Prioress' Tale

The Prioress' prologue is simply a prayer to the Virgin Mary, worshipping God, and asking her to help the narrator properly to tell of God's reverence, and to guide the tale as it is told.

The Prioress' Tale

Once in an Asian town, there was a Jewish ghetto at the end of a street, in which usury and other things hateful to Christ occurred. The Christian minority in the town opened a school for their children in this city at the other end of the same street. Among the children attending this school was a widow's son, an angelic seven year old who was, even at his young age, deeply devoted to his faith. At school he learned songs in Latin, and could sing his *Ave Marie* and *Alma redemptoris*, a song giving praise to the Virgin Mary, and pay due reverence to Christ.

As he was walking home from school one day singing his *Alma redemptoris*, he provoked the anger of the Jews of the city, whose hearts were wasps' nests made by Satan. They hired a murderer who slit the boys' throat and threw the body into a cesspit.

The widow searched all night for her missing child, begging the Jews to tell her where her child might be found, but they refused to help her or give her any information. Jesus, however, gave her the idea to sing in the place where her son had been cast into the pit: and as she called out to him, the child, although his throat was slit, began to sing his *Alma redemptoris*. The other Christians of the city ran to the pit, amazed at what was happening, and sent for the provost.

The provost praised Christ and his mother, Mary, and had the Jews tied up. The child was taken up and carried, in a great and honorable procession to the nearest abbey, his corpse singing all the while. The local provost cursed the Jews, and ordered their death by hanging. Before the child was buried, holy water was sprinkled onto him, and he began to speak. The abbot of the abbey questioned him as to how he could sing, and the child answered that the Virgin Mary had placed a grain on his tongue that allowed him to speak. The abbot took this grain from his tongue, allowing him to die, and finally pass on to heaven. The child was buried in a marble tomb as a martyr, and the tale ends with a lament for the young child, but also for "Hugh of Lyncoln" (a real child martyr, slain by Jews in Chaucer's day).

Analysis

The Prioress' Tale is overtly a "Miracle of the Virgin", a reasonably common Christian genre of literature which represents a tale centered around Christian principles and a devotion to the Virgin Mary, but within the warm affection that the Prioress shows for her Christian faith is a disquieting anti-Semitism immediately obvious to the modern reader in our post-Holocaust times.

The tale is an unabashed celebration of motherhood, and an unapologetic argument for the virtue of Christianity over Judaism, and in most critics' readings, it partly serves as a grim reminder that anti-Semitism by no means began with Hitler in the Second World War. The guiding figure of the tale is the Virgin Mary, addressed directly in its prologue, who serves both as the exemplar for Christian values and as the intervening spirit who sustains the murdered child before he passes on to heaven. Her mortal parallel is the mother of the murdered boy, who dearly loves her son and struggles to find the boy when he is lost.

The Tale itself, as Seth Lerer has pointed out is "a nightmare of performance..." which "dramatizes just what happens when a performer faces a hostile audience". The little clergeoun of the tale (the child) is an unsuspecting victim, murdered solely because of his eagerness to sing: one of many tales which seems to take as its theme the danger of speaking, the potential danger of words and language, and a warning about what happens to people who open their mouths at the wrong moment (other such tales include those of the Manciple and the Nun's Priest).

Despite its interest in song and performance, the key question still seems to be whether we are to read the tale as an outdated example of anti-Semitism, acceptable to a medieval audience but acceptable no longer or whether there is another option. If there is, it probably lies in the sentimental presentation of the Prioress' Tale, and the juxtaposition of the extremely angelic singing seven year old, and the extremely cruel and horrible Jews (who even go to the lengths of throwing the child's corpse into a cesspit). If we remember that the Prioress is a woman so sentimental that she even cries over a dead mouse, it's quite a contrast in her personality that she expends such vitriol over the Jews. Perhaps there is some sort of contrast; perhaps the Prioress is intended to be held at arm's length from Chaucer. The bottom line with this tale is that it entirely depends on your reading of the details.

Summary and Analysis of Chaucer's Tale of Sir Thopas

Prologue to the Sir Thopas

When the Prioress' Tale was done, every man in the company looks serious, having heard of the miracle she described. Until the Host, beginning to joke, turns to Chaucer himself ("he looked upon me") and asks him what sort of man he is, as he is always looking at the ground. "Looke up murily", the Host tells Chaucer, calling him a doll ("popet") and describing him as elvish-faced. The Host then demands that Chaucer tells a "tale of myrthe", and "that anon" (do it soon). Chaucer replies to the Host that he only knows one tale: a rhyme that he learned many years before.

The Tale of Sir Thopas

(I)

Asking the "lords" to listen, the tale announces itself as being "of myrthe and of solas" (fun and seriousness). It then introduces Thopas, a fair knight with a white face, rose-red lips, blond hair and beard, and a seemly nose. Thopas was very well dressed and he could hunt for deer, go hawking, and he was a good archer. Many maidens were brought in for him to sleep with, but he was chaste, and no lecher.

One day Thopas went out riding on his gray horse, carrying a launcegay and a longsword, and passed through a forest which had many wild beasts in it (buck as well as hares). Thopas heard the birdsong and fell into a love-sickness, and rode so fast that his horse sweated. Thopas therefore lay down to give him and his horse a rest, deciding that he would be in love with an elf-queen.

Thopas then climbed back into his saddle to find an elf-queen, but he came across a great giant called "Sire Olifaunt", who threatened Thopas that, if he left his territory, he would kill his horse. Thopas (described as "the child") said that he would meet with the giant tomorrow, as he had forgotten his armor, and travelled in the opposite direction very fast. This giant threw stones at him, but he got away.

(II)

"Yet listeth" (keep listening) to my tale, the narrator continues, because Thopas has again come to town. He commanded his merry men, as he had to fight a giant with three heads. They gave him sweet wine and gingerbread and licorice, and then Thopas got dressed in his armour. The end of this fit tells the company that if they "wol any moore of it" (want to hear any more) then the narrator will try to oblige them.

(III)

"Now holde youre mouth, par charitee" (Now shut up, for charity's sake) begins the third fit, before explaining that Thopas is of royal chivalry. Thopas drank water from the well with the knight Sir Percivel, until one day…

Here the Host "stynteth" [stops] Chaucer's Tale of Thopas

No more of this, for God's sake, says the Host, criticizing the "rym dogerel" which Chaucer uses. Chaucer asks why he has had his tale stopped when it is the best rhyme he knows – and the Host replies that his crappy rhymes are not worth a turd, advising him rather to tell something in prose. Chaucer obliges, promising "a litel thyng in prose", finally asking the Host to let him tell "al my tale, I preye".

Analysis

Sir Thopas offers up one of the funniest moments in the Canterbury Tales. Written in ridiculously bouncy tail rhyme, the poem is a hilarious parody of Middle English verse romances packed full of bizarre pastoral details. Thopas, for example, is hugely effeminized, well-dressed, and with a girl's name (Thopas was usually a woman's name in the medieval period). Thopas falls in love, in the manner of the courtly knight, before he has decided who he will be in love with (an elf-queen, in the end) and runs away from his climactic battle at the end of the first fit because he has forgotten his armour.

In the Ellesmere manuscript, the setting of Sir Thopas has the tale ever vanishing into the margin, and close readers will note the way each fit is half the length of its predecessor - there is, as well as its "dogerel" parody of verse romance, a definite sense that Chaucer the character has definitely run out of things to say. Note the number of times Chaucer has to ask the company to listen or to be quiet (implying perhaps the jeers and responses of a less-than-impressed pilgrim audience) and note too the way that details from the prologue seem to echo in the Tales: an effeminized, antisocial Chaucer becomes an effeminized, entirely chaste Thopas, the Host's comment that Chaucer looks like he would find a "hare" becomes a forest with hares for wild beasts, an "elvish" looking-Chaucer inspires the "elf-queen who is to be Thopas' lover. To that, we might add, a storyteller Chaucer reluctant to tell a tale (but pushed into the spotlight) becomes a knightly Thopas desperate to escape knightly combat. The apparent purposeless of the narrative, packed with pointless details, might well reflect a narrator who is making the tale up as he goes along.

There are several interpretable jokes hidden in the fabric of the tale. Chaucer is parodying his own endless inventiveness, celebrating his own skill at creating varied voices, by presenting himself as someone who cannot even come up with a single bearable story – and, silenced by his own characters, the abortion of Chaucer's tale actually points to a remark about the strength of his characterization. Chaucer's characters, it seems, are so well written that they give advice about tale-telling to their writer. Sir Thopas, vanishing fit by fit as it does, also demonstrates Chaucer's awareness of his own elusiveness, the self-vanishing quality which enacts the invisibility of the writer's point of view – which we have already mentioned in several other tales. The Chaucer sent into the fiction to represent the author is, we and he know all too well, a poor imitation of the real thing - but it is the nearest thing to an omniscient author we are going to get.

Summary and Analysis of Chaucer's Tale of Melibee

The Tale of Melibee

There was once a young man named Melibee, mighty and rich, who had with his wife Prudence, a daughter called Sophie. One day he took a walk into the fields, leaving his wife and daughter inside his house, with the doors shut fast. Three of his old enemies saw it, and, setting ladders to the wall of his house, entered, beating his wife, and giving his daughter mortal wounds in five places: "in hir feet, in hire handes, in hir erys, in hir nose, and in hir mouth" (972).

When Melibee returned and saw what had happened, he was like a madman, tearing his clothes, weeping and crying. Prudence, his wife, stopped his tears, and gave him some useful advice from various authorities. Prudence eventually advised him to call a group of people to come to him, to explain to them what had happened, and listen to their counsel.

As per his wife's instructions, Melibee took counsel from "the grete congregacioun of folk", and the advice falls into two camps. The surgeons, physicians, lawyers, and the old urge caution, and a considered reaction, but his neighbors and "yonge folk" urge war.

Melibee wants to wage war, and Prudence urges haste - there follows an argument about who should prevail, and Prudence, eventually, triumphs. She tells Melibee that he should choose his counselors carefully, and to set their advice against their – apparent and hidden - motives. Prudence then, at length, goes through all of the advice that Melibee has been given and shows him that open war is not a good option, for a variety of moral, ethical, and practical reasons.

Prudence interprets the attack on Sophie as the damage done to her because of man's vulnerability to the World, the Flesh, and the Devil. Her remedy: negotiate peace and leave all to God's grace and forgiveness.

The three enemies who have performed the deed are found and brought before Prudence, who suggests forgiving them; Melibee again argues for a fine, which she again argues him out of. Melibee forgives them, and, delighted with himself, praises at length his own generosity.

Analysis:

Don't worry if you've never read Melibee in full - a very famous academic (who I shall leave nameless) studying at one of the world's most renowned universities once admitted to me that she'd never made it right through either. Melibee, first and foremost, seems to be a punishment for cutting Chaucer off mid-flight with Sir

Thopas; before beginning it, he promises a "litel thyng in prose", asks that he is not interrupted, and then delivers a hugely lengthy tale of almost unsurpassed dullness. If one saw in Thopas running from the giant the figure of Chaucer trying to escape the Host's demand, Melibee seems to represent him coming back with the armor.

Some critics have also argued that an omission Chaucer deliberately makes from its source, Renaud de Louens' *Livre de Melibee et de Dame Prudence* [after 1336] (itself a translation of Albertanus of Brescia, *Liber consolationis et consilii*) [1246]) points to Melibee as a separate composition intended for the recently-crowned Richard II. Among Melibee's many pieces of advice, Chaucer omits, significantly for a child-king, "Woe to the land that has a child as king". Is this, perhaps a manual for a king?

Melibee is also rather self-consciously a construction; a patchwork of proverbs, sayings and wise words, some of which have already appeared in the tales, and none of which are likely to be entirely original. Part of the reason for its length is that its characters constantly cite authority after authority to justify their opinion – and this academic arguing inflates the thin plot of the tale into page after page of citation and quotation. So keen is everyone to get their favorite authority into the argument that we never even find out what happens to mortally-wounded Sophie.

Melibee is, like Thopas (improvised from its situation), a text made up of text – and it proves (particularly if the Parson's tale, the only other tale in prose, was a late addition to the Canterbury project) Chaucer's mastery of genre, if nothing else. Prose tracts, full of academic discussion rather than dramatic, narrative progression, are not without of his ability.

Within the tale itself, Prudence is another example of the patient and long-suffering wife who demonstrates her virtue through stoicism, and, like Constance, her name is an obvious signifier of one of her prominent qualities (Sophie, the daughter, has a name meaning "wisdom"). Her role in the story is not as an active agent, she is a passive influence on the other characters; and she is a good example to consider in examining the issue of "female counsel", raised hitherto but particularly in the Nun's Priest's Tale. Melibee suggests, above all, that women are worthy counselors and interpreters, and, although the tale celebrates Prudence, its title is apt - it points to Melibee himself, a man able to learn from his wife, whose name means "sweet learning" or "sweet knowledge".

Summary and Analysis of The Monk's Tale

Prologue to the Monk's Tale

When Chaucer's tale of Melibee has finished, the Host says (for the second time) that he wishes his wife could hear the tale of Prudence and her patience and wise counsel: his wife, he goes on to extrapolate, is an ill-tempered shrew. Turning to address the Monk, he bids him be 'myrie of cheere', and asks whether his name is John, Thomas or Albon, asking which house he is of. Admiring the Monk's skin and stature, the Host jokes that he could be a good breeding fowl, if only he were allowed to breed! Religion, the Host goes on, has taken up all the best breeding people, and left just the puny creatures to populate the world.

The Monk takes all this joking well, and promises a tale (or two, or three) of the life of Edward the Confessor, but first, announces he will tell some tragedies, of which he has a hundred stored up. Tragedy, as the Monk defines it, is a story from an old book of someone who fell from high degree and great prosperity into misery, and ended wretchedly; tragedies are also usually presented in hexameters, he thinks.

The Monk's Tale

The Monk's tale is a collection of tragedies, designed to advise men not to trust in blind prosperity but be aware that Fortune is fickle and ever-changing.

Lucifer is the first tragedy told, who fell from an angelic heaven down to Hell. **Adam** is next, the one man not born of original sin, who was driven from Paradise.

Sampson's tale is told at greater length, explaining how he fell from grace when he admitted his secret to his wife, who betrayed it to his enemies and then took another lover. The story is that Samson slew one thousand men with an ass's jawbone, then prayed for God to quench his thirst. From the jawbone's tooth sprung a well. He would have conquered the world if he had not told Delilah that his strength came from his refusal to cut his hair. Without this strength his enemies cut out Samson's eyes and imprisoned him. In the temple where Samson was kept he knocked down two of the pillars, killing himself and everyone else in the temple.

Hercules' tragedy is next. Hercules' strength was unparalleled, but he was finally defeated when Deianera sent Hercules a poisoned shirt made by Nessus.

Nabugodonosor (also spelled Nebuchadnezzar), was the king of Babylon who had twice defeated Israel. The proud king constructed a large gold statue that he demanded his subjects pray to or else be cast into a pit of flames. Yet when Daniel disobeyed the king, Nebuchadnezzar lost all dignity, acting like a great beast until God relieved him of his insanity.

The next tragedy is about Balthasar, the son of Nebuchadnezzar, who also worshipped false idols. He had a feast for a thousand lords in which they drank wine out of sacred vessels, but during his feast he saw an armless hand writing on a wall. Daniel warned Balthasar of his father's fate. Daniel warned him that his kingdom would be divided by Medes and the Persians. **Balthasar**, according to the Monk, exemplifies the way that Fortune makes friends with people before making enemies with them.

Cenobia (or Zenobia), who was beautiful and victorious in war, is the next tragic hero of the tale. The queen of Palmyra refused the duties of women and refused to marry, until she was forced to wed Odenathus. She permitted him to have sex with her only so that she could get pregnant, but no more. Yet the proud woman, once Odenathus was dead, was defeated by the Romans and paraded through Rome bound in chains.

King Pedro of Spain, subject of the next story, was cast from his kingdom by his brother. When attempting to regain his throne, Pedro was murdered by this brother.

Peter, King of Cyprus, is the next subject; he brought ruin on his kingdom and was thus murdered.

Other tragedies include **Bernabo Visconti**, who wrongly imprisoned his nephew. **Ugolino of Pisa**, a count, was imprisoned in a tower in Pisa with his three young children after Ruggieri, the bishop of Pisa, had led a rebellion against him. His youngest son died of starvation, and out of his misery Ugolini gnawed on his own arms. The two children that remained thought that Ugolini was chewing himself out of hunger, and offered themselves as meals for him. They all eventually starved. **Nero** did nothing but satisfy his own lusts and even cut open his own mother to see the womb from which he came. He had Seneca murdered for stating that an emperor should be virtuous. When it appeared that Nero would be assassinated for his cruelty, he killed himself. **Holofernes** ordered his subjects to renounce every law and worship Nebuchadnezzar. For this sin Judith cut off Holofernes' head as he was sleeping.

The Monk next tells of Antiochus Epiphanes, who was punished by God for attacks on the Jews. God made Antiochus infested with loathsome maggots. The Monk then admits that most have heard of Alexander the Great, poisoned by his very own offspring. He follows with the tale of Julius Caesar, who had Pompey murdered but was himself assassinated by Brutus. The final story is of Croesus, King of Lydia, the proud and wealthy king who was hanged.

All of these tales are simply re-tellings of the popularly known stories: all focus on the same theme of people of high degree falling into misery or death. Finally the Monk's Tale is interrupted.

Analysis:

The Monk provides one of the first-known definitions of tragedy in English literature, and, though his tale might have been fascinating to Chaucer's medieval audience, many of whom would not know the classical stories it largely details, it does not receive a huge amount of attention or adoration from modern readers and critics.

The Monk's tragedies are drawn from a variety of sources: Biblical, classical, historical and even some that, in Chaucer's time, would have been within reasonably recent folklore and memory. Yet the model of tragedy that the Monk offers is not, in fact, a classical model as such, but a Boethian one - a reminder of the mutability of life itself, and the tendency of fickle, feminine Fortune to spin her wheel and bring those at the top crashing down to the ground. It is, on one level, simply a series of car-crash narratives - an unrelenting dark, Boethian reminder that the high-status end miserably.

Some more recent studies have tried to locate the Monk's tale, with its emphasis on the stories told about the history, and its focus on the writers from whom the Monk has drawn the stories, as a response to Boccaccio's *De casibus* tragedies and a comment on the involvement of writing, poets and poetry in the support of tyrants and despots.

Yet neither of these readings of the Tale really explains what it is doing within its context. Louise Fradenburg argues very persuasively in her book that the Monk is a death's head at the feast - a sudden explosion of misery and death into the festive fun of the Canterbury project. The Monk's own solid physical reality, good for breeding (so the Host jokes - and breeding is the opposite of dying) is juxtaposed with his tales, precisely about the end of the body and its death, rather than life and strength.

Moreover, the numbers that the Monk quotes - he has a hundred tragedies in his cell, of which he manages to fit in seventeen before he is interrupted - suggest a painfully dismal repetition of the fall from fortune to misery, fortune to misery, fortune to misery. It is rather as if the Monk himself becomes a sort of anti-Canterbury Tales all of his own: each of his mini-tales progressively darkening the horizon.

It is no wonder then that the Knight sees fit to interrupt the Monk and halt his tale - particularly as the Monk tells tales largely about the demise of high-status characters (and the Knight, of course, is the pilgrimage's highest-ranking pilgrim). The Monk himself presents a threat to the fun of the tale: he is all 'ernest' and no 'game', as the Host points out to him, and - beginning a trend which arises more and more as these final tales progress - when he is interrupted, he refuses to speak any further. One of the tellers has his mouth firmly closed.

Summary and Analysis of The Nun's Priest's Tale

The Prologue of the Nun's Priest's Tale

Here the Knight "stynteth" (stops) the Monk's Tale

"Hoo!" says the Knight, "good sire, namoore of this". The Knight then praises the Monk, but says that he has heard quite enough about mens' sudden falls from high status and grace, and would far rather hear about men climbing from poverty to prosperity.

The Host steps in to concur, telling the Monk that his tale is boring the company, and that his talk is worth nothing, because there is no fun to be had from it. The Host asks the Monk to tell another tale - and the Monk responds that, having no desire to play and have fun, he has said all he has to say. The Host then turns to the Nun's Priest, asking him to draw near, and asking him to be merry of heart in his tale. "Yis, sir", says the Nun's Priest – and, described as a "sweete preest" by the narrator, the Nun's Priest begins his tale.

The Nun's Priest's Tale

A poor widow, rather advanced in age, had a small cottage beside a grove, standing in a dale. This widow led a very simple life, providing for herself and her daughters from a small farm. In a yard which she kept, enclosed all around with palings and with a ditch outside it, she had a cock called Chaunticleer, who was peerless in his crowing. Chaunticleer was beautifully coloured, with a comb redder than coral, and a beak as black as jet, and he had under his government seven chickens, who were his paramours, of which his favourite was Dame Pertelote.

One morning, Chaunticleer began to groan in his throat, as a man who was troubled in his dreams does, and Pertelote, aghast, asked him what the matter was. Chaunticleer replied that he had had a bad dream, and prayed to God to help him to correctly interpret it. He had dreamt that he, roaming around the yard, saw an animal "lyk an hound" which tried to seize his body and have him dead. The "hound's" colour was somewhere between yellow and red, and his tail and both his ears were tipped with black.

Pertelote mocked him, telling him that he was a coward. Pertelore then argues that dreams are meaningless visions, caused simply by ill humors (bad substances in the body) – and quotes Cato at length to demonstrate her point. Her solution is that she will pick herbs from the yard in order to bring his humors back to normal.

Chaunticleer disagreed, arguing that while Cato is certainly an authority, there are many more authorities available to be read who argue that dreams are significations

– of good things and bad things to come. He stated the example of one man who, lying in his bed, dreamt that his friend was being murdered for his gold in an ox's stall, and that his body was hidden in a dung cart. Remembering his dream, this man went to a dung cart at the west gate of the town, and found the murdered body of his friend. Chaunticleer then described the story of two men, who were preparing to cross the sea. One of them dreamed that, if he crossed the sea the next day, he would be drowned - he told his companion, who laughed at him, and resolved to go anyway. The ship's bottom tore, and his companion was drowned. Chaunticleer also cited the examples of Macrobius, Croesus and Andromache, who each had prophecies in their dreams.

Then, however, Chaunticleer praised Pertelote, asking her to speak of "mirth", and stop all this talk of prophecy - the beauty of her face, he says, makes him feel fearless. He then quoted the proverb "Mulier est hominis confusio", translating it as "Woman is man's joy and all his bliss", when it actually translates "Woman is man's ruin". Chaunticleer then flew down from his beam, called all of his hens to him, and revealed that he'd found a grain lying in the yard. He then clasped Pertelote to him with his wings, and copulated with her until morning.

When the month of March was over, Chaunticleer was walking in full pride, all of his wives around him, when a coal fox (a fox with black-tipped feet, ears and tail) broke through the hedges and into the yard. He bode his time for a while. The narrator then goes off into an aside, addressing Chaunticleer, and wishing that he had taken "wommennes conseils" (woman's counsel) – before he moves back into the tale, reminding us that his tale "is of a cok".

Chaunticleer sang merrily in the yard, and, casting his eyes among the cabbages, caught sight of the fox – and would have fled, but the fox addressed him, asking where he was going, and claiming to be his friend. The fox claimed to have met Chaunticleer's mother and father, and talked of his father's excellent singing voice, and the way his father used to stretch out his neck and stand on his tiptoes before singing. The fox then asked whether Chaunticleer can sing like his father – and Chaunticleer stood on his tiptoes, stretched out his neck, closed his eyes, and, as he began to sing, the fox grabbed him by the throat and ran off to the wood with him.

The poor widow and her two daughters, hearing the cry of the chickens, ran after the fox toward the crove, and many other men and animals ran after them. Chaunticleer managed to speak to the fox, and encouraged him to turn to his pursuers and curse them, telling him that he was going to eat the cock. The fox agreed – but as he opened his mouth to agree, the cock broke from his mouth suddenly and flew high up into a tree. The fox tried to persuade him down, saying that he had been misinterpreted, and that Chaunticleer should fly down in order that he might "seye sooth" (tell the truth) about what he had meant, but Chaunticleer knew better this time. The fox finally cursed all those who "jangleth whan he sholde holde his pees" (chatters when he should hold his peace).

The narrator then addresses everyone who thinks the tale is mere foolery, asking them to take the moral of the tale, rather than the tale itself: taking the fruit, and letting the chaff remain. Thus ends the Nun's Priest's Tale.

Epilogue to the Nun's Priest's Tale

The Host, praises the tale as "myrie", and then, as he did with the Monk, suggests that the Nun's Priest would be an excellent breeding man (trede-foul) if only he were allowed to breed - for the Nun's Priest, the Host continues, is brawny, with a great neck and large chest.

Analysis

The Nun's Priest's Tale is one of the best-loved and best-known of all of the Tales, and one whose genre, in Chaucer's time and now, is instantly recognizable. It is a beast fable, just like Aesop's fable, and as one of Chaucer's successors, the medieval Scots poet Robert Henryson, would go on to explore in great detail, its key relationship is that between human and animal. The key question of the genre is addressed at the end by the narrator himself: telling those who find a tale about animals a folly to take the moral from the tale, disregarding the tale itself. But can we take a human moral from a tale about animals? Can an animal represent – even just in a tale – a human in any useful way?

For a start, it is important to notice that the animal-human boundary is blurred even before the tale begins, when the Host mocks the Nun's Priest (who, being a religious man, would have been celibate) and suggesting that he would have made excellent breeding stock (a "tredefowl", or breeding-fowl, is the word he uses). The thought is an interesting one – because if we can think of the Nun's Priest himself as potentially useful in breeding, animalistic terms, then can we think of his tale in potentially useful in human terms?

The question frames the other themes of the tale. The issue of woman's counsel is raised again (last foregrounded in Chaucer's tale of Melibee) explicitly – should Chaunticleer take Pertelote's advice about how to interpret his dreams? Should he disregard his dreams, and get on with his life? He does, of course, looking among the cabbages (perhaps even to find herbs), when he sees the fox – and at that point, the tale seems to suggest, he should never have listened to his wife in the first place: his fears were valid.

That is, until we remember what the narrator tells us anyway at a crucial point, that his tale is "of a cok" – about a chicken. It is hardly as if we need a prophetic dream to tell us that foxes like eating chickens: its what we might call animal instinct. This is doubly highlighted when, after quoting Cato and discussing the various textual politics of dream interpretation, Chaunticleer calls his wives excitely to him because he has found a grain of corn – and then has uncomplicated animal sex with Pertelote all night. It is a contradiction, Chaucer seems to imply, to expect unchicken-like behavior from a chicken: yet the contradiction is one which fuels the whole genre of beast fable. If the Nun's Priest had too much human dignity and restraint to be a breeding fowl, Cato-quoting Chaunticleer has animal urges too strong to be a viable auctour.

Except that, of course, with the possible exception of Arviragus and Dorigen in the Franklin's Tale, there is no more stable and robust "marriage" in the Canterbury Tales than Chanticleer and Pertelote's. The two fowl have a fulfilling sexual relationship - and the sex occurs as a pleasurable, uncomplicated end in itself, a stark contrast with the sexual transactions of the Franklin and the Wife of Bath's tales. In one sense, then, the animals are not so bestial.

Interpreting dreams, incidentally, is a favorite theme of Middle English literature, and it frames a whole genre of poetry, known as "dream poems", of which Chaucer himself wrote several (including the Book of the Duchess and the House of Fame). Dreams and text are closely intertwined, and – even in this tale – the way in which a dream poem juxtaposes the text of the dream with the text of the story is clear. Is a dream any more or less real than a tale? If we can take a moral from a tale, can we take one from a dream?

This tale is in many ways a return to the ground, a return to basics. We start with a poor widow, and a dusty yard - a setting far removed from the high-culture classical tragedies of the Monk. Moreover, the tale keeps emphasizing anality and bottoms - in Chaunticleer's two examples of dreams-coming-true, a dung cart and a breaking ship's "bottom" are the hinge of the story, and Pertelote's advice to Chaunticleer is to take some "laxatyf" to clear out his humours. There is a good-natured sense of groundedness about this tale, a return – after the dark run of Monk (interrupted), before him the punishing Melibee (and interrupted Sir Thopas) and bitter Prioress – to the humour and warmth of the early tales. Yet its theme also darkly foreshadows the end of the tale-telling project itself.

If the tale, taken simplistically, does endorse prophetic dreams (though, as mentioned above, a look at the animal nature of its characters might be seen as parodying the whole concept!) then what is the "moral" that the narrator wants us to take away at the end? As ever, this isn't totally clear. Yet one thing it might be is the importance of speaking or not speaking.

One of the things that makes Chaunticleer the morally-representative chicken a problem is the fact that he can speak and argue with his wife on the one hand, yet cry "cok! Cok!" when he sees a grain on the floor. He is both chicken and human, rather like Chaucer writes as both himself and as Nun's Priest. The tale, however, is structured by people knowing when to speak and not knowing when to speak: Pertelote speaks out to wake Chaunticleer from his dream, Chaunticleer foolishly opens his mouth to sing for the fox when he is captured, and it is Chaunticleer's final visitation of the trap that he himself fell into on the fox which causes him in turn to open his mouth – and let Chaunticleer go. Know when you should "jangle" (chatter) and know when to hold your peace.

It is a theme of course which points a sharp finger at the whole idea of a beast fable - the whole genre, we might argue, resting on the writer precisely ignoring the correct moments to have a character speak or not speak; and it also is a dangerous moral for the Tales as a whole. In a work of literature that constantly apes orality, the injunction to shut up is a serious one – and, as a comparison of the Nun's Priest's Tale to the Manciple's Tale reveals – one very much in Chaucer's mind at the very end of the Canterbury project.

Summary and Analysis of The Second Nun's Tale

The Second Nun's Prologue

The tale, written in rime royal, begins with an invocation for people to avoid sin and avoid the devil, and then a formal invocation to the Virgin Mary.

There then follows an interpretation of the name of St. Cecilia, the subject of the Second Nun's Tale: in English, the narrator tells us, her name might be expounded as "heaven's lily". The lily might represent the chasteness of Cecilia, or indeed, her white honesty. Or, perhaps her name would be best read as "the way toward understanding", because she was an excellent teacher, or perhaps a conjoined version of "heaven" and "Lia". Cecilia, the prologue concludes, was swift and busy forever in doing good works.

The Second Nun's Tale

Saint Cecilia was by birth a Roman and tutored in the ways of Christ. She dreaded the day that she must marry and give up her virginity. However, she came to be engaged to Valerian. On the day of their wedding, underneath her golden robes, she wore a hairshirt, praying to God that she might remain undefiled.

On their wedding night she told a secret to Valerian: she had an angel lover who, if he believed that Valerian touched her vulgarly, would slay him. Valerian said he would believe her if he could see this angel, and she told him to go to the Via Appia and find Pope Urban among the poor people. Once Urban purged him of his sins, Valerian would be able to see the angel. When he reached Via Appia, Urban suddenly appeared to Valerian and read from the Bible. Another old man, clad in bright white clothes, with a gold-lettered book appeared before Valerian, asking him whether he believed what Cecilia had told him. When he said he did, Pope Urban baptized Valerian and sent him back home.

Returning home, he found the angel with Cecilia. This angel had brought two crowns of flowers from Paradise that will never wilt, and gave one to Cecilia and one to Valerian. The angel claimed that only the pure and chaste would be able to see this crown. Valerian then asked for the angel to bless his brother and make him pure.

This brother, Tibertius, came and can smell, but not see the flowers. Valerian explained his new faith, and eventually tried to persuade his brother to be baptized. Tibertius, however, did not like the idea of being baptized by Urban, whom, he said, would be burnt if people ever found him. Valerian told his brother not to fear death, because there was a better life elsewhere. Cecilia explains the Holy Trinity and other key tenets of Christianity to him, and afterwards, Tibertius agrees to accompany the couple to Pope Urban.

Tibertius was baptized and became a perfect Christian – and for some time the three lived happily, God granting their every request. However, the sergeants of the town of Rome sought them, and brought them before Almachius the prefect, who ordered their death. During their execution, one of the sergeants, Maximus, claimed that he saw the spirits of Valerian and Tibertius ascend to heaven. Upon hearing this, many of the witnesses converted to Christianity. For this Almachius had him beaten to death, so Cecilia had him buried alongside Valerian and Tibertius.

Almachius summoned Cecilia, but she refused to appear frightened of him, or bow to his power; and when she was given the choice of forego Christianity or perform a sacrifice, she refused both of her options. She refused to admit any guilt and condemned Almachius for praising false idols. He ordered that she be boiled to death, but she, despite being left all day and night in a bath with fire underneath it, stayed cold – she did not even break a sweat.

Almachius then commanded his servant to slay her in the bath, and, though he struck her three strokes in the neck, he could not decapitate her, and she lay there half-dead. Christians stopped the blood with sheets, and, although she lay there for three days in agony, she never stopped teaching them the Christian faith. She even preached to them, giving them her property and her things, and – after three days – she died, and her body was taken to Pope Urban. He buried her by night among the other saints, and consecrated her church, still worshipped to this day as the church of St. Cecilia.

Analysis

The Second Nun's Tale is a conventional religious biography, a "saint's life", as the medieval genre it belongs to is often called. Written in rime royal, it is very likely that Chaucer composed the tale previous to and separate from the Canterbury project, and only adapted it to fit within the Tales later. The Second Nun tells the story of Saint Cecilia in a dry, sanctimonious fashion that exalts her suffering and patient adherence to her faith, and, in a fashion that might be compared to the Prioress' and the Clerk's tales, stresses the patent inhumanity and saintliness of Cecilia from the first moment.

Like the "litel clergeoun" of the Prioress' tale, Cecilia transcends the horrors of the mortal world: she stands against paganism, against false idols, and even against death, and is rewarded by being translated into a saint at the end of the tale. Some critics have recently begun to compare this tale to the Canon Yeoman's tale which follows it, wondering whether Cecilia herself might undergo some sort of transformational alchemical process: though she, unlike the false Canon's trick-coals, is entirely unchanged when heated up.

The tale points to the mythological nature of medieval Christianity. The metaphor of the angelic floral coronets, which only Christians can see, for example, is a physical manifestation of the idea that Christians belong to a City of God, a distinct community with shared values that exists within a secular and often hostile environment. There is perhaps also an interesting thought lurking in the tale about the problematic contradiction (highlighted by the Host in his words to the Monk and the Nun's Priest) that human ministers of God are not allowed to be sexual beings: Cecilia, of course, sets herself apart from the earthlier women of the Tales (the Wife of Bath is the key example) by, right at the start of the tale, professing her distaste for sex.

Summary and Analysis of The Second Nun's Tale

Summary and Analysis of The Canon's Yeoman's Tale

Prologue to the Canon's Yeoman's Tale

With the story of Saint Cecilia finished, the company continues on its journey until two men overtake them. One was clad all in black but with a white gown underneath – a Canon - and his horse sweated as if it ridden for three miles. The horse that rides underneath the Canon's Yeoman similarly sweated so much that it could hardly go further. The Canon (the first man) greets the company warmly, and explains that he had hoped to join them; his Yeoman too is extremely courteous.

The Host asks if the Canon can tell a tale, and his Yeoman responds that he knows more than enough about mirth and jollity – and adds that, if the Host knew the Canon as well as he does, he would wonder how he could do some of the things he can. The Canon is, the Yeoman says, a "passyng man" (an outstanding, [or *sur*-passyng man). The Host guesses that his master is a clerk, but the Yeoman says that he is something greater, telling him that he could pave all of the ground from here to Canterbury in silver and gold.

The Host is quite amazed, but then asks why – if the Canon is so important - he cares so little for his honor, and dresses so shabbily. The Yeoman seems initially horrified at the question, but then adds in secret that the Canon believes that overdone dress-sense is a vice. The Host asks where the Canon lives, and the Yeoman tells him that it is in hiding places and the back lanes of the suburbs of a town. The Host then turns to the Yeoman himself, asking why his face is so discolored. The Yeoman explains that is because he spends his time blowing in the fire – and then reveals that the Canon and he spend most of their time doing "illusioun", borrowing money, promising profit and then slipping away.

While the Yeoman was talking, the Canon drew near and heard everything – and chastised

him, telling him to hold his peace, and warning him that he was revealing things that should not be revealed. The Host bids the Yeoman to tell on, and when the Canon realized that the Yeoman would not be silenced, he fled. Since his lord is gone, the Yeoman concludes, he will tell the company everything he knows.

The Canon Yeoman's Tale

(*Prima pars*)

With this Canon, the narrator begins, I have lived for seven years, and yet I am no closer to understanding his science. The "slidynge science", as he calls it, has made him only poor – and, so he argues, it will do to anyone who applies himself to it. The narrator then expounds in detail the processes of alchemy, with reams of scientific terminology, rehearsing an inventory of vessels made of pottery and glass, apparatus like curcurbites and alembics, and minerals like arsenic and brimstone.

The narrator then recites the four spirits (volatile substances – which are easily evaporated by heat) and the seven bodies (metals) which, in medieval alchemy, were an almost forerunner to the periodic table. No-one who practices alchemy, the narrator concludes, will profit: he will lose everything he puts into it. No matter how long he sits and learns the terms, he will never gain from it. The narrator then turns on God, saying that though God had given them hope and they had worked hard to discover the philosopher's stone, they had had no luck.

Alchemists, the narrator continues, are liars. The narrator then tells of the reactions some of the metals produce - shattering pots, sinking into the ground, and leaping into the roof; and, he says, when a pot explodes, his master just throws away the elements (even when someone points out that some of the metal has survived) and starts again, despite the money that people have spent to buy the goods. The narrator reveals that – despite any arguments about why the pot might have shattered – the alchemists always seem to get it wrong. Finally, the narrator claims that nothing is what it themes: apples which look nice are not good, men that seem the wisest are the most foolish, and the man who seems most trustworthy is a thief.

Et sequitur pars secunda

This is the tale proper of the Canon's Yeoman, and it tells of a Canon whose infinite falsehood and slyness cannot be written. He makes anyone he communicates with behave foolishly, and yet people ride for miles to make his acquaintance, not knowing or suspecting that he is a charlatan.

The narrator then makes a slight aside to apologise to canons in general, claiming that his tale is of one bad canon, but is not representative of all canons, just as Judas was the one traitor among the apostles.

In London, there lived a priest who sung masses for the dead – and one day he was visited by the false Canon, who begged him to lend him a certain amount of gold. The priest obliged him, and, three days later, the Canon returned to pay him back. Expressing gratitude that the Canon has paid him back on time, the priest prompts a speech from the Canon about the importance of "trouthe" and keeping one's word. The Canon then promises to show the priest some of his "maistrie" before he goes. The narrator then comments on the falsehood and dissimulation of the Canon, before apparently addressing the audience of the pilgrimage: "This chanon was my lord, ye wolden weene?" (This canon was my master, you think?). No – this Canon, the narrator tells us, is another Canon, and, even in describing him, the Yeoman's cheeks blush red.

The Canon sent the priest's servant to bring quicksilver and coals, and then took a crucible and showed it to the priest, telling him to put an ounce of quicksilver in there. The priest did as he asked, and they put the crucible into the fire. Yet the false Canon took a fake coal, unseen, which had a hole in it, stopped with wax, which held silver filings. While the priest was wiping the sweat from his face, laid the coal in the furnace just above the crucible. Naturally, the wax melted and the silver filings ran out over the crucible.

Next, the Canon told the priest to bring him a chalk stone, promising to make a gold ingot of the same shape. The Canon slyly inserted a metal rod into the chalk, and, when he threw into a bowl of water, the chalk melted away leaving only the silver rod. The priest was delighted, but the Canon decided to prove himself once more. Taking another ounce of quicksilver, the Canon took up a hollow stick, filled at one end with silver filings, and, putting it above the bowl of quicksilver, made it seem as if the silver (from the stick) had been translated from the quicksilver.

Thus by various tricks and schemes, the Canon filches the money from his unsuspecting audience, and charges them huge amounts for his wisdom and his trickery. Moreover, by telling the priest that, if he (the Canon) were caught, he would be killed as a sorcerer, the Canon secured still higher prices for his services.

It is easy, the narrator concludes, for men to take the gold they have and turn it into nothing. Moreover, after cataloguing some authorities (including Arnaldus of Villanova, Hermes Trismegistus, and Plato) who wrote of the philosopher's stone, the narrator firmly concludes that God does not want men to know how to get it – and therefore, we should "let it goon". If God does not want it discovered, so it should remain.

Analysis

The Second Nun's Tale is hardly over, when two new characters arrive on the pilgrimage, sweatily riding up behind the pilgrimage and eventually overtaking them. The arrival of the Canon and his Yeoman is such an unusual event – particularly at this point of the Canterbury Tales – that the compiler of the Hengwrt manuscript (see "The texts of the Tales" for more information on the manuscripts) actually left it out altogether. It is an unusual construction, and one with "transformation" and "change" as its central themes - not surprisingly, then, it pins down a change already starting to occur within the fabric of the Tales as a whole.

Alchemy is the subject of the Canon Yeoman's tale, as he calls it, the "sliding" science: and alchemy argues that all things are in a state of perpetual change, slipping from one thing to another. Coals can become the philosopher's stone, metal melts to become a false covering for a crucifix, and thanks to the trickery of the tale's false Canon, we are never quite sure what substance it is we are examining. Can we ever tell what it is we are looking at – can we ever know the difference between true and false?

The Canon himself is a mysterious, imposing and peripheral figure, and one who, at the very moment his falsehood appears to be rumbled, runs away from the company, and from the Tales – for good. He is almost silent, and yet his silence is not (like Chaucer's) from shyness, or from high-status - clad in a hooded black robe, with a glimpse of white underneath, he even physically appears shrouded and covered up. Moreover, we never actually ascertain whether the Yeoman's tale is about this Canon, or – as he claims – about another Canon. It seems hugely improbable, even to take the Yeoman's words at face value (and the tale offers other warnings about doing that!), that the Yeoman would have this amount of knowledge about an entirely different Canon. The Canon then is a liminal figure, sitting somewhere on the border between reality and fiction, between true and false.

His Yeoman too starts his literary life as his advocate: praising the Canon as an extraordinary, wonderful, skilled man, before immediately retracting all that praise (almost without any provocation) to unmask his master as the tricky charlatan he is. Yet this casts huge doubt on the veracity of what the Yeoman actually utters - there is a big difference between his initial claim that the Canon could pave the way to Canterbury with gold, and the portrait of the Canon built up in his tale. Moreover, the sweating arrival of the pair (their horses are so wet that they can hardly move), combined with the all-black Canon and blushing-red Yeoman suggests that even the characters within the frame narrative of the Tales are undergoing some sort of alchemical transformation. There is a sliding transformation in what the characters actually say and think – but this is backed up in the visual metaphor of them being physically "slydinge."

The central image of the Canon Yeoman's tale is the devilish furnace at the center of their back-street workshop, and (rather like the alchemical/furnace imagery in Jonson's *The Alchemist*) it is a complex metaphor: for hell, for devilish behavior – and falseness, but also for money. As the Pardoner argued in his tale, money is the root of all evil: and yet, unlike the slight comeuppance the Pardoner is served with by the Host at the end of his tale, justice is entirely absent from the denouement of the Canon Yeoman's tale. The last furnace we saw in the Tales was Gervays' in The Miller's Tale – a timely reminder, perhaps, of the neat interclicking justice of Absolon's branding Nicholas. Neither the Canon nor his Yeoman receive any sort of narrative punishment.

Yet the way that this timely reminder of the profitability of falsehood intrudes upon the Tale also points to the complex narrative problem of the Pardoner's tale: just in the way that the Pardoner's hollow words and empty bones could bring people to salvation, so too can the Canon's trickery actually make him money – and, moreover, the Canon's Yeoman can supposedly turn this experience into a moral tale for the company to listen to. Of what substance is a tale made? Can a tale acknowledge the desire for gold and the ingenuity of the misdemeanors of those who pursue gold without endorsing them? As it is reaching its conclusion, the pilgrimage is waylaid by another pertinent reminder of the tale-telling project and its questionable substance. Tales, as Chaucer will admit in the retraction, and language, are not always innocent.

Summary and Analysis of The Manciple's Tale

Prologue to the Manciple's Tale

The Host turns to the sleeping cook, and asks whether any man might be able to wake him. Awaking, pale and unalert, the Cook proclaims that he would rather sleep than have some of the best wine in Cheapside. The Manciple steps in courteously, excusing the cook, and then mocking him – his open mouth, which the devil could put his foot in, his stinking breath – to his face for his drunkenness. The Cook is furious, but too drunk to speak, and promptly falls off his horse. Everyone lifts him up out of the mud, and the Host addresses the Manciple, telling him that the Cook is too drunk to tell a tale, and has more than enough to do keeping himself out of the mud and on his horse.

However, adds the Host, it is a folly to openly mock the Cook to his face, for one day he might have his revenge, and "quit" the Manciple's words. "No", says the Manciple, and produces a draught of wine, which he gives to the Cook to drink, with the result that the Cook thanks him generously. Everyone is much amused, and the Host comments that good drink turns rancor into love, blessing Bacchus, god of wine. He then asks the Manciple to tell his tale.

The Manciple's Tale

When Phoebus, god of poetry, lived on earth, he was the lustiest of bachelors, a superior archer and the envy of all for his singing and playing on his musical instruments. Phoebus kept in his house a white crow, which could imitate the speech of any man, and who could sing more beautifully than a nightingale.

Phebus also had a wife, whom he loved more than his own life, and did his best to please her and treat her courteously – except that he was extremely jealous, and so would watch her suspiciously. Guarding a wife so closely, the narrator reminds us cynically, is pointless – if she is faithful, there is no need to do so, but if she is unfaithful no amount of monitoring will keep her faithful. Take any bird, he says, and put it in a cage – and no matter how gilded the cage and how good the treatment, the bird would still twenty thousand times rather go and eat worms in a forest. Animals, the narrator insists, can never be trained to be unanimalistic. So do men, the logic continues, always have a lecherous appetite to sleep with someone socially lower than their wives. Flesh is fond of novelty.

This Phoebus, though he had no idea of it, was deceived: his wife had another man, "of litel reputacioun", hardly worth comparing with Phoebus himself. One day when Pheobus was away, she sent for her "lemman" (lover – a word the narrator takes some pains to reject having said). The white crow saw their "working" together, and said nothing until Phoebus returned home, when the crow sang "Cokkow! Cokkow!"

(Cuckold! Cuckold!). Pheobus initially thought the bird sang a song he did not recognize, but the crow clarified that his wife had had sex with a man of little reputation on his bed.

Phoebus thought his heart burst in two – he took his bow, set an arrow to it and murdered his wife, and for sorrow of that, destroyed his harp, lute, cithern and psaltry, snapping too his arrows and his bow. Then he turned to the crow, calling it a traitor, mourning his wife, and accused the crow of lying to him - and then, to "quite anon thy false tale", pulled out every one of the crow's white feathers, made him black and took away his song and his speech, slinging him out of the door and leaving him to the devil. It is for this reason that all crows are black.

The narrator turns to his audience, and tells them to be aware of what they say - never tell a man that he is a cuckold because he will hate the messenger. One must think on the crow and hold one's tongue.

Analysis

There is something hugely destructive – and self-destructive – about this tale, and particularly the way it takes the god of poetry, himself a plausible representative for the whole idea of the Tales themselves, and turns him into a petty, jealous murderer. The Manciple's Tale is almost painfully brief - not given to flights of fancy, we are given the simple information – jealous husband, unfaithful wife, talking crow, and then destruction, of wife, of crow, and of poetry.

The Manciple's Tale is also a cousin, though a darker cousin, of the Nun's Priest's Tale, and it seems likely, at least, at first, that a tale about a talking crow and the mythical god of poetry will be another fantastical beast fable – the genre leads us to expect the happily ending exploits of another Chaunticleer. Yet what actually happens is a bitter shift in tone - the happy, metaphorical beginning of the tale falls through into a painful reality. The god of poetry is a jealous human, and the white-feathered beautiful-voiced talking crow becomes the black, hollow-voiced harbinger of doom of reality. The tale brings the reader back to earth with a bump, and its reminder is clear: know when to fall silent. Know when not to speak, when not to tell.

And "tell" is an appropriate verb to raise - like Chaucer himself, the crow can counterfeit the speech of every man. The crow, in other words, is a veritable Canterbury poet himself - and what this tale teaches him, through physical suffering, is that some subjects are simply not to be told. Chaucer, in the Retraction, raises the worry that the Tales are sinful or blasphemous, and the moral "hold your tongue" could not simply be the message of the final Tales, but a thought a nervously religious Chaucer was increasingly coming to find in his own mind. Telling, in other words, has its limits - and it is better to stop before there are real consequences to it. As the final real "tale" (discounting the Parson's sermon) of the Tales, it makes for a bleak, but unmistakable end.

Summary and Analysis of The Parson's Tale and Chaucer's Retraction

The Parson's Prologue

By the time the Manciple's tale had finished, the sun had set low in the sky. The Host, pronouncing his initial degree fulfilled, turns to the Parson to "knytte up wel a greet mateere" (conclude a huge matter) and tell the final tale. The Parson answered that he would tell no fable – for Paul, writing to Timothy, reproved people who turned aside from the truth and told fables and other such wretchedness.

What the Parson promises is morality and virtuous matters - and jokes that he does not know of the alliterative poetry tradition of the South. He leaves his tale, he says, to clerks, for he himself is not "textueel". Everyone agreed that it was the best way to end the project, and asked the Host to give the Parson the instruction to tell the final tale. The Host did so, hasting the Parson to tell his tale before the sun went down.

The Parson's Tale

The Parson's tale is not actually a tale as such, but a lengthy medieval sermon on the subject of penitence. The first part of his sermon defines the three parts of penitence – contrition, confession and satisfaction, and expounds at length (with several biblical examples) the causes of the contrition.

The second part of the sermon considers confession, which is the truthful revelation of the sinner's sin to the priest. Sin is then explained as the eventual product of a struggle between the body and soul for dominance of a person – and therefore there are two types of sin: venial (minor, smaller sins) and deadly (serious sins).

The third part of the sermon considers each of the seven deadly sins as branches of a tree of which Pride is the trunk. Pride is the worst of the sins, because the other sins (Ire, Envy, Sloth, Avarice, Gluttony and Lechery) all stem from Pride. Each sin's description is followed by its spiritual remedy – and the Parson states the rules for oral confession.

There are a number of conditions to penitence, including the intensity of the sin committed, the haste to contrition and the number of times the sin was committed. The fruit of this penitence is goodness and redemption in Christ. Following this short return to the subjects of penitence (and satisfaction), the final lines seem to suggest, by way of images of the sun and the morning, a vision of Paradise: bodies which were foul and dark become brighter than the sun, the body, formerly sick and feeble, becomes immortal and whole, and in a place where no-one feels hunger, thirst or cold, but is replenished by the perfect knowledge of God. This paradise, the final lines of the tale conclude, is only attainable through spiritual poverty and by avoiding sin.

Retraction: "Heere taketh the makere of this book his leve"

The narrator, speaking in the first person, prays to everyone that reads this "litel tretys" (little treatise – probably the Parson's tale) that, if they like anything they read in it, they thank Jesus Christ. If they find anything that displeases them, moreover, they are to put it down to the narrator's ignorance, and not to his will – he would have written better, if only he had the cunning.

The narrator then asks the reader to pray for him that Christ has mercy on his sins and forgives him in his trespasses, and particularly of his translations of worldly vanities: the book of Troilus, the book of Fame, the book of the twenty-five ladies, the book of the Duchess, the book of the Parliament of Birds, and the tales of Canterbury – those that "sownen into synne" (tend toward sin).

However, the narrator thanks Christ for his translation of the Boece and other books of saint's legends and homilies, hoping that Christ will grant him grace of penitence, confession and satisfaction, through the benign grace of the King of Kings, so that he may be "oon of hem at the day of doom that shulle be saved" (one of them at the day of doom who shall be saved).

The book ends with a short Latin prayer and Amen, before announcing that the book "of the tales of Caunterbury, compiled by Geffrey Chaucer" has ended, adding "of whos soule Jhesu Crist have mercy".

Analysis

One of the biggest questions about the Tales as a whole is precisely how they end. Throughout his works, and even within the Tales (look, for example, at the interruptions of Sir Thopas and the Monk's tales) Chaucer proves that he knows how to create a false ending, a trick ending, which ends by not ending, by not concluding. The Canterbury Tales ends on a decidedly pious and religious note, first with the Parson's lengthy sermon, and then with a retraction written as "Chaucer". The Parson's sermon, a translation from a medieval work designed to advise clergy in the salvation of souls, would be a plausible medieval sermon – there seems nothing in it that is ironic: it is a perfect example of its genre.

Yet can the Parson's sermon seem anything other than just another genre? In a work which has anthologized genres – we have already read beast fables, saint's lives, fabliaux, Breton lays, and all manner of other stories – and problematised them, drawing attention to their speaker's voice as something (as the Pardoner points out) ventriloquized, can we really be expected to take the Parson's voice seriously?

Critics disagree wildly about the answer to this question. The same problem applies to Chaucer's retraction – which, as in the Man of Law's prologue, blurs the line between the Chaucer writing the Tales (who has also written the Book of the Duchess, Troilus and Criseyde, and so on) and the fictional Chaucer who is a character within the pilgrimage. Is the Chaucer who writes these tales just another constructed voice?

Or, perhaps, is the Retraction of the tales a genuine one? Chaucer, in this theory, genuinely was dying and was unable to finish the work – or for some reason, felt the need to immediately retract it, as he genuinely believed that it did come too close to sin. Thus, before the Host's plan was complete, he concluded the tale with a pious sermon and then a Retraction: no-one could therefore accuse the Tales of being unchristian. Is it a death-bed confession?

A Retraction is a fairly usual way for a medieval work to end, and perhaps that points us to the aforementioned effect: its very normality is perhaps a clue that Chaucer's intention is not pure and simple. For it could be read simply as another "funny voice" – the voice of the Chaucer who told Sir Thopas: could be read as comedy rather than penance. Moreover, as E.T. Donaldson has firmly stated, the use of the Parson's Tale as an interpretative key to unlock the whole of the Tales is problematic, particularly when you consider the deliberate religious provocation of tales like the Miller's, the Wife of Bath's and the Merchant's. The tales by no means seem to be written to a purely Christian agenda - though Christianity is undoubtedly a key theme.

End-points in Chaucer are difficult to definitively interpret, and perhaps this dichotomy was intended by Chaucer himself. Perhaps this ending is simply one way of closing down the Tales – the Manciple's tale, of course, has been only the most recent in a line of tales which reiterate the advice of these final fragments to hold one's peace, and know when to fall silent. Is this Chaucer, on an imaginary, real or literary deathbed, punningly, holding his peace, but also being "at peace"? One thing is for sure: understanding the ending of the Tales seems a fitting encapsulation of the complex problem of interpreting the work as a whole.

Summary and Analysis of The Parson's Tale and Chaucer's Retraction

Suggested Essay Questions

1. **The Prioress wears "a brooch of gold ful sheene / On which ther was first write a crowned A, / And after *Amor vincit omnia"* (General Prologue, l.159-162). Might "Love Conquers All" be the moral of the Tales?**

   This question asks you to consider the Tales as a whole work, and to trace the theme of love conquering all throughout the work. Remember that with a question like this, it is just as possible to disagree as to agree: just make sure you justify your answer with examples from the text.

   Useful tales to look at might include *The Miller's Tale, The Merchant's Tale, The Prioress' Tale, The Manciple's Tale, The Wife of Bath's Tale.*

2. **Choose one word (and its variants), and use it as a key to the interpretation of any one Tale.**

   This question asks you to follow the fortunes of a single word through any tale, and structure your argument around the repeated uses of this single word. You should start by highlighting all the moments in the tale that the single word appears, and talk about how its meaning changes or deepens as the tale progresses.

   Useful tales to look at might include *The Miller's Tale* (suggested word: "pryvetee"), *The Wife of Bath's Tale* (suggested word: "clooth"), *The Franklin's Tale* (suggested word: "trouthe"), *The Shipman's Tale* (suggested word: "tail") or *The Merchant's Tale* (suggested word: "corage").

3. **What do women most desire in the Tales?**

   This question asks you to look at the characterization and presentation of the female characters in the Tales (which could include characters within tales as well as female pilgrims). Remember to begin by examining the Tale from which the question comes.

   Useful tales to look at might include: *The Wife of Bath's Tale, The Miller's Tale, The Merchant's Tale, The Shipman's Tale, Melibee.*

4. **"The Wife of Bath is Chaucer's most completely drawn character." Do you agree?**

   This question asks you to compare the characterization of the Wife of Bath to any of the other characterizations in the Tales. Do you think the Wife is completely drawn? If so, why? If not, why not - and which character is better fleshed out?

   Useful tales to look at must include *The Wife of Bath's Tale.*

5. **"Men in the Tales are largely depicted as idiots, blindly and foolishy adhering to outdated, impractical codes of chivalry and honour." Do you agree?**

This question asks you to consider the presentation of men in the Tales. Look at examples which support the quotation's argument, but also remember that Chaucer includes a variety of presentations - and that there is certainly justification in the text for taking the opposing view to the quotation.

Useful tales to look at might include *The Knight's Tale, The Merchant's Tale, The Physician's Tale, Sir Thopas, The Franklin's Tale.*

6. **"Chaucer writes the Tales in pairs". Do you agree?**

This question asks you to consider the structure of the Tales, and consider whether each Tale has a pair. It would be a good idea to examine some tales which do fall naturally into pairs, but also to consider some that do not - or perhaps, even fall into threes.

Useful tales to look at might include *The Miller's Tale* with *The Knight's Tale* or *The Reeve's Tale, The Friar's Tale* with *The Summoner's Tale, The Shipman's Tale* with *The Wife of Bath's Tale* and *The Manciple's Tale* with *The Nun's Priest's Tale.*

7. **"It is no wonder that Chaucer retracts the Tales at the end of the work. They are quite simply blasphemous." Can we read the Tales as a religious work?**

This question asks you to consider the theme of religion in the Tales. It is a difficult subject to precisely consider, and would be helped by some knowledge of the religious context of the later 1300s when Chaucer was writing. Don't forget to define "blasphemy".

Useful tales to look at might include: *The Miller's Tale, The Wife of Bath's Tale, The Summoner's Tale, The Prioress' Tale, The Second Nun's Tale, The Parson's Tale.*

8. **"Women in Chaucer are idealized objects of desire." Write an essay about the presentation of women in the Tales.**

This question asks you to consider the presentation of women across the Tales as a whole. Remember to include contradictory facets: there is nothing to say that Chaucer's writings are consistent from tale to tale. It might be best to choose two entirely contradictory examples (say, Cecilia in the Second Nun's Tale, and the Wife of Bath) and try and find some points of similarity.

Useful tales to look at might include *The Wife of Bath's Tale, The Prioress' Tale, The Miller's Tale, The Reeve's Tale.*

9. **At what point does a joke become cruel? Write an essay about one Tale of your choice.**

This question asks you to look at the comedy of the Tales and to decide whether you find it funny or cruel (or a combination of the two). Consider whether physical harm is funny, whether cruelty and comedy depend on events depicted or on presentation, and on how dissimilar tales are which you find very funny, and very cruel.

Useful tales to look at might include *The Miller's Tale, The Reeve's Tale, The Summoner's Tale, The Manciple's Tale, The Physician's Tale, The Wife of Bath's Tale and The Merchant's Tale.*

10. **"Chaucer, though he features himself in the Tales, is adept at vanishing completely." Write an essay about the persona(e) of Chaucer.**

This question asks you to focus on what you learn about Chaucer himself: remember that there are two Chaucers, one a character, one the author.

Useful tales to look at might include *Sir Thopas, Melibee, The Man of Law's Tale, The General Prologue, the Retraction.*

11. **"What nedeth wordes mo?" Is language worthless in the Canterbury Tales?.**

This question asks you to write an essay about language in the Tales, and analyse whether or not you think it is presented as having value, as being worthless, or - more likely - that it is some combination of the two.

Useful tales to look at might include *The Reeve's Tale, The Manciple's Tale, The Nun's Priest's Tale, The Knight's Tale, Chaucer's Retraction.*

Literature in the Middle Ages

Chaucer was famous in his own times not for being an author, but for being a civil servant, and it is important to realize that the medieval conception of an "author" was very different from the modern one. An "auctour", to a Middle English reader, was not someone living now, but (usually) a dead classical writer, whose works had already had massive influence on the literary landscape of the day. Very often medieval poems come down to us anonymous – and not simply because of lost information or incomplete manuscripts. Some medieval authors felt that their name was unimportant, because they were only re-telling an "auctour's" work.

Chaucer, like Shakespeare, draws heavily on existing texts, on his favorite authors (usually Boccaccio or Boethius) and on well-known stories to make up the fabric of the Canterbury Tales: unlike our modern idea of writing a novel, there was no sense that originality mattered. Text was something interpretable, flexible, changeable – and which was passed on in new ways from generation to generation.

Alan de Lille famously commented that "auctorite" (authority – being an author) had a wax nose: a brilliant metaphor for the way a text could be interpreted one way and then the other – led, in short, in entirely contrasting directions. Moreover, the "glossing" tradition, by which commentary was applied directly to a text, was rife at the time Chaucer was writing, and the idea that a text could be shaped heavily by the gloss put onto it (see, for example, the Wife of Bath's railing against clerics) was very current.

Text and cloth (via the Latin "textere" – "to weave") were considered images of each other: representing not only the way that a cloth can be used to obscure reality, present a "version" of it, but also the way that cloth, like text, can be manipulated into entirely different shapes. "Cast up the curtyn", says the lothly lady at the end of the Wife of Bath's tale, but – as that tale demonstrates – it is impossible in Chaucer to know precisely when you have got all of the text/cloth out of the way, and you are looking at the real thing.

One very famous drawing of Chaucer (pictured) shows him reading to an assembled crowd, and it is certainly possible that the transmission of his works would partly be through being read aloud, whether at court or otherwise in public. Works of literature, before the printing press had been invented, had to be copied out by hand by a scribe, and Chaucer's famous poem addressing his scribe, Adam Scriveyn, is an interesting indicator of the way this method could lead to the spread of inaccuracies:

"So ofte a daye I mot thy werke renewe

It to corecte and eke to rubbe and scrape;

And al is thorugh thy neglygence and rape."

which translates as follows

"So many days I have to re-do your work

To correct it, and to rub and scratch mistakes out

And all because of your negligence and rashness".

The oral tradition of literature represented within the pilgrimage, then, could also be considered a crucial part of the life of the text itself: the tale-telling game, in fact, a representation of the way the work itself would gain purchase on an audience.

It is worth knowing about authority, about glossing, and about the joint oral-written nature of a text in Chaucer's day: all three themes are brought to bear on the interpretation of the tales in this ClassicNote, and all of them are explored in some details by Chaucer within the Tales themselves.

The Texts of the Tales

Scholars do not know whether the Tales we have are a complete text, and the textual history of the Tales is long and checkered. The first printed edition, printed by William Caxton in 1478, was based on a manuscript now lost, and the 82 manuscripts which survive include 14 perfect (or nearly perfect) copies containing all of the Tales, 41 which are very nearly complete, only missing a few pages, 7 copies which are very fragmentary, and 20 which contain a single tale or a single passage deliberately cut out of the larger work. No manuscript can be dated within Chaucer's lifetime, meaning that every manuscript was written between 1400 and the time of Caxton's printing press (just less than a century later).

There are two basic camps into which these manuscripts fall into: and these two differing texts of the Tales are known as the **Ellesmere** and the **Hengwrt** manuscripts respectively.

The Ellesmere manuscript contains the most complete text of the Tales that we have, written in a large, clear book hand which covers 232 leaves of fine quality thin vellum, printed on unusually large pages with unusually generous margins. Famously, the main attraction of the manuscript is the lavish illumination, illustration and decoration: huge, golden and colorful initials joined to elaborate borders appear on seventy-one pages. Facing the first line of each of the Tales is an illustration of its narrator (the very famous illustration of Chaucer is featured opposite).

The Hengwrt manuscript of the Tales is less complete than the Ellesmere, and its tales are in a different and unique order. The manuscript, made of vellum, is in poor condition, stained, and with vermin having eaten about 9cm from the outer corners of its pages. However, its text is very regular, and is therefore now used by most modern editors. As the dialect, spelling and paleography are similar to that in Ellesmere, some critics have argued that the same scribe wrote both manuscripts. One final difference is that only the first page of Hengwrt has a pink and blue full vinet border: unlike Ellesmere, the rest of the pages are undecorated.

However, although the order featured in Ellesmere is more usually followed by editors, the text of Hengwrt is considered to be better, and so printed editions often feature a largely Hengwrt-based text ordered according to Ellesmere.

Why are the texts so different? Nobody is sure. Hengwrt, we know, was put together extremely quickly, and some scholars believe it was a hurried edition rushed to press in order to quickly get the Tales into print. Perhaps when Ellesmere was made, some years later, the papers were more carefully scrutinized, better ordered, and some extra material which had come to light (who knows how!) could be included. That said, it is perfectly possible that the two manuscripts represent different periods of Chaucer's work on the Tales: the Ellesmere capturing a late (potentially the last) stage of revision before the end of Chaucer's work on the project, potentially due to

Chaucer's death in c. 1400.

The different orders of the manuscripts (explaining too which Tales feature in which fragment) is below:

Ellesmere

Fragment 1 (General Prologue, Knight, Miller, Reeve, Cook)

Fragment 2 (Man of Law)

Fragment 3 (Wife of Bath, Friar, Summoner)

Fragment 4 (Clerk, Merchant)

Fragment 5 (Squire, Franklin)

Fragment 6 (Physician, Pardoner)

Fragment 7 (Shipman, Prioress, Sir Thopas, Melibee, Monk, Nun's Priest)

Fragment 8 (Second Nun, Canon's Yeoman)

Fragment 9 (Manciple)

Fragment 10 (Parson, Retraction)

Hengwrt

Fragment 1

Fragment 3

Fragment 2

Squire's Tale (without Prologue)

Squire-Franklin Link as 'Merchant's Prologue'

Merchant's Tale

Merchant's Epilogue – Squire's Prologue (without break) as 'Host's Words to Franklin'

Franklin's Prologue and Tale

Second Nun's Tale

Clerk's Prologue, Tale and Epilogue

Fragment 6

Fragment 7

Fragment 9

Fragment 10

Sources: The Roman de la rose

The *Roman de la Rose* was probably the most famous, and certainly one of the most influential poems of the Middle Ages. It was begun by Guillaume de Lorris in 1237, but – for some reason - left incomplete at line 4058: although the poem does seem to be heading toward a finishing-point, it is usually presumed that Guillaume died before finishing it. A poet whose name has not survived then supplied the text with a quick 78-line ending, but it was later in the century that Jean de Meun took it in hand and wrote three times more than the text he had started with, taking the line count to 21,780.

The poem therefore falls into two distinct halves. The first 4058 lines (written by Lorris in c. 1230) simply describe the attempts of a courtier to woo the woman he is in love with, represented here as an allegory, "Rose", which is both a female name and a pertinent (floral) metaphor. The poem is set in a walled garden, the inside of which represents love and romance, and the outside, normal "realistic" life. The additional 17,724 lines which Jean de Meun added are quite different in character, more philosophical, more misogynistic, far more sexual, and (significantly) "Rose" shifts from an abstract idealism to a character with physical, sexual and sensual reality. The "Rosebud" the courtier desires then, is a strange, shifting symbol: sometimes the woman, sometimes her sexual organs, sometimes her virginity, sometimes her love. More recently, scholarship has begun to construct arguments for the essential unity of the work; precisely how it was viewed by many medieval readers.

That Chaucer knew the *Roman de la Rose* is certain, and its influence can be felt across his own works. The poem is styled as a dream vision (of which Chaucer himself wrote several), and its focus on love, on women, and on female sexuality can be seen reflected in several of the Tales. Moreover, the dream vision's focus on interpreting allegory: the distance between a metaphorical character within the fictional world and the meaning of that character to the reader in the "real world" is also inherited and complicated by Chaucer in the Tales. Many, many specific and general influences from the text can be seen in the Roman de la rose, from large borrowings like La Vielle, the original Wife of Bath (who speaks many of the same lines!) to smaller borrowings like the details of the Prioress' table manners.

Central too to the shift in authors of the *Roman de la Rose* is the shift from the representation of the female love object as an idealized, courtly, beautiful abstraction to a real, sexualized, human. Clearly, in reading the Miller's, Reeve's, Wife of Bath's and Shipman's Tales (to name but a few) the dichotomy between these two presentations of the female in the Middle Ages is preserved and highlighted by Chaucer in the Tales.

Sources: The Roman de la rose

Sources: The Decameron

Giovanni Boccaccio (1313 – 1375) along with Dante (who went before him) and his contemporary Francis Petrarch (the source of the Clerk's Tale of Griselde), is one of the three greatest and best known poets of the Italian fourteenth century. Chaucer certainly knew the writings of all three poets, and perhaps met both Petrarch and Boccaccio (more likely Petrarch, but potentially both).

Boccaccio's *Decameron*, a long work compromising several shorter tales, is often thought to be the main stylistic influence on the Tales, though there is no evidence that Chaucer ever read it as an entire work. The Tales as a whole, however, do owe much to Boccaccio: the Knight's Tale is based on *Il Teseida* and Chaucer's "heigh style", as Larry Benson has commented, "owes something to Boccaccio's attempt to emulate the classics in his own vernacular." The Monk's Tale draws on Boccaccio's works in Latin, and the Clerk's, Franklin's, Merchant's, Pardoner's, Reeve's and Shipman's Tales all have analogues (or at the very least, stories with considerable similarities) in Boccaccio's *Decameron*.

Sources: The Decameron

Sources: Fabliaux

Fabliau is the singular, and fabliaux the plural, and a fabliau is clearly and simply defined by Larry Benson in his introduction to the Riverside Chaucer:

> "A fabliau is a brief comic tale in verse, usually scurrilous and often scatological or obscene. The style is simple, vigorous, and straightforward; the time is the present, and the settings real, familiar places; the characters are ordinary sorts... the plots are realistically motivated tricks and ruses. The fabliaux thus present a lively image of everyday life among the middle and lower classes. Yet that representation only seems real... the plots, convincing though they seem, frequently involve incredible degrees of gullibility in the victims and of ingenuity and sexual appetite in the trickster-heroes and -heroines.

(The Riverside Chaucer, p. 7.)

Fabliaux was primarily a French genre, and many examples still survive; there are very few fabliaux from Chaucer's time written in English.

The Tales of the Miller, Reeve, Shipman, Summoner and Cook are all fabliaux, and many of the other tales, including the Merchant and the Wife of Bath, demonstrate the influence of the genre. Further reading in fabliaux might included Guèrin's Bèrenger of the Long Arse and the fabliaux of Marie de France, who seemed to parody her own writings in courtly love by writing fabliaux about the deceptive nature of women.

Characteristic of the fabliaux genre is its dangerousness and irreverence, often twinned in Chaucer with an almost-blasphemy:

> "The cuckoldings, beatings, and elaborate practical jokes that are the main concern of the fabliaux are distributed in accord with a code of "fabliau justice," which does not always coincide with conventional morality: greed, hypocrisy, and pride are invariably punished, but so too are old age, mere slow-wittedness, and, most frequently, the presumption of a husband, especially an old one, who attempts to guard his wife's chastity... The fabliau, in short, is delightfully subversive - a light-hearted thumbing of the nose at the dictates of religion, the solid virtues of the citizenry, and the idealistic pretensions of the aristocracy and its courtly literature, which the fabliaux frequently parody, though just as frequently they parody lower-class attempts to adopt courtly behavior."

(The Riverside Chaucer, p. 8.)

Author of ClassicNote and Sources

Robert William, author of ClassicNote. Completed on November 20, 2008, copyright held by GradeSaver.

Updated and revised Soman Chainani November 30, 2008. Copyright held by GradeSaver.

Geoffrey Chaucer (ed. Larry D. Benson). The Canterbury Tales (in The Riverside Chaucer). Oxford: Oxford University Press, 1987.

Carolyn Dinshaw. Chaucer's Sexual Poetics. Wisconsin: University of Wisconsin Press, 1989.

E. Talbot Donaldson. Speaking of Chaucer. New York: Norton, 1970.

Jill Mann. Feminizing Chaucer. Rochester, NY: D. S. Brewer, 2002.

Jill Mann. Chaucer and Medieval Estates Satire: The Literature of Social Classes and the General Prologue to the Canterbury Tales. Cambridge: CUP Archive, 1973.

Seth Lerer et al. The Yale Companion to Chaucer. Yale University: Yale University Press, 2007.

Geoffrey Chaucer (ed. Barry Windeatt). Troilus & Criseyde: a new edition of Chaucer's The book of Troilus. University of Michigan: Longman, 1984.

Helen Cooper. The Structure of the Canterbury Tales. . Athens: University of Georgia Press, 1984.

Robert P. Miller. Chaucer: Sources and Backgrounds. Oxford: OUP, 1977.

L. O. Aranye Fradenburg. Sacrifice Your Love . Minnesota: University of Minnesota, 2002.

Essay: "Love" in the Courtly Tradition

by Anonymous
May 03, 2000

In the "Franklin's Tale," Geoffrey Chaucer satirically paints a picture of a marriage steeped in the tradition of courtly love. As Dorigen and Arveragus' relationship reveals, a couple's preoccupation with fulfilling the ritualistic practices appropriate to courtly love renders the possibility of genuine love impossible. Marriage becomes a pretense to maintain courtly position because love provides the opportunity to demonstrate virtue. Like true members of the gentility, they practice the distinct linguistic and behavioral patterns which accompany the strange doctrine of courtly love. The characters' true devotion to the relationship becomes secondary to the appearance of practicing the virtues of truth, honor, and generosity. After establishing the inverted hierarchy of values, Chaucer paints a bleak picture of the potential for love and relationships in a world in which a distinction needs to be made between secular and private roles. Dorigen differentiates between "hir housbonde" and "hir love" (250) and Arveragus distinguishes between "his lady" and "his wyf" (125).

Immediately, Chaucer signals the practice of chivalric courtship as the knight who is of noted "heigh kinrede" (63) ceremoniously completes the "many a labor" (60) of a courtly lover. The description of the duties that must be undertaken by a classic courtly lover seeking a wife for social fulfillment corruptss the image of courtship being motivated by the existence of true love. The emphasis on the inconvenience with which Arveragus, "dide his payne" (57) suggests he performs "many a greet empryse" (59) out of obligation and convention rather than as a part of a genuine amorous pursuit. The weakly disguised presence of the "ye" in each of these words announces Arveragus' awareness of the eyes of the courtly audience observing his performance. The concern with the outward appearance of the relationship extends to Dorigen as she dutifully accepts his proposal as a means of repaying the "distresse" (65) undergone by her lover. The brief description of the couple's courtship covers only 13 lines, suggesting that the relationship's foundation has little time to progress beyond the preliminary stages of lusty, physical attraction before the marriage is instated.

Framing the already bleak portrayal of this "accord," (69) a word typically used to refer to business agreements or compromises, is the contractual terminology of their agreement which further downplays the emotional foundation of the relationship. Instead, the negotiated terms that "frendes everich other moot obeye" (171) indicate that the lovers are settling for amicable companionship. The agreement itself is ridden with contradictory terms trying to reconcile the tensions between the inner sphere where passionate love resides and the outer sphere which operates under the codes of courtly love. The two agree that Arveragus will be her "Servant in love, and lord in merrage" (121), but the in reality these two social positions are mutually exclusive, indicating the impossibility of the success of this relationship. One of the two will have to be the dominating figure for it to survive, but then this will eliminate the possibility of love which "wol nat ben constreyned by maistrye" (92). The "lawe of love" (126) in the medieval period mandates that a husband is the lord of his wife, and Arveragus grants her sovereigty only within the scope of their private life because he must uphold the tradition of male domination in the outside world. Arveragus' promise to becomes a way to demonstrate that " [p]acience is a heigh vertu" (101). Always aware of the connection between his actions and his rank he states, "Save that the name of soveraynetee, / That wolde he have for shame of his degree." (79-80). If the two truly were in love, these sorts of issues would not need to be settled or would even arise because a couple would assume that a wife would be true to her husband and that he would treat her with respect and honor. Instead, marriage is being used to further one's opportunity to perform noble and virtuous roles, explaining the struggle between a lover's commitment to his personal or public life. Chaucer foreshadows the improbable success of this duality with the Dorigen's proclamation, "Ne wolde never God bitwixe us tweyne" (171). Not only does this contain a double negative, suggesting that a force will indeed disrupt this arrangement, but the phraseology also indicates that their relationship will be without God who should be a uniting force in any marriage.

Chaucer takes pains to mention that "[t]he joye, the ese, and prosperity" (132) of their relationship last only a "yeer and more" (134). Chivalric love's preoccupation with appearances impels behavior that stymies the success of love. In addition to the previously noted irony of a lover undergoing a painful courtship to win his desired object, Arveragus undertakes additional burdens under the charade of being a good lover. Chaucer criticizes the requirements of courtly love by placing such pursuits directly at odds with their objects. Arveragus self-imposes a two-year separation from Dorigen is an effort "to seke in armes worshipe and honour." (139). Why must a husband leave his wife to prove he is worthy of her love? His decision to leave his bride after only a year of marriage suggests the value he places upon success in the public eye overrides the need to be attentive to his private affairs. In fact, Arveragus pursues this task with more enthusiasm than he shows in any of his interactions with this wife. "Perhaps the "lust he sette in swich labour" (140) indicates Arveragus' preference to be a warrior lover in the public sphere instead of a servant in his private sphere. On the battlefield, he can through virile performance release some of the sexual frustrations which develop from the constraints in his marriage. Assuming this is true, his departure represents a revolt against his powerless position in his marriage.

Dorigen strengthens the possibility of marital bliss existing only as a pretense when she pines away for her husband not as one would secure in the belief that he will return to her, but as if she is apprehensive about his desire to voluntarily leave the battlefield. He sends her "lettres hoom of his welfare," (166) establishing that her worries extend beyond mere concern with his health. Although Dorigen's reaction to the separation from her husband is marked by her profound sense of grief, there seems to be a melodramatic insincerity in her response. She weeps "as doon these

Essay: "Love" in the Courtly Tradition

noble wyves whan hem lyketh," (146) suggesting her mourning is a ploy to win her friends sympathies and their attentions to "every confort possible in this cas" (154). Perhaps she is behaving in concert with the belief that true lovers suffer from a physical and emotional malady, amor hereos. Her belief that "with good hope lete hir sorwe slyde" (175) further establishes the facade of grief is easily replaced with a face of good cheer when it befits her interests.

The already weak links in this marriage culminate in Aurelius' pursuit of Dorigen. The very fact that Aurelius undertakes the methods of a courtly lover in an attempt to covet another man's wife implies that in this courtly environment the sacred vows of truth in marriage are commonly corrupted by adultery. Although Dorigen rejects his advances and pledges to grant him her love only if he performs a task she deems impossible, it shows the fault of a society operating under a system where relationships exists only when they fulfill predetermined conditions. If Dorigen faithfully enters her promise of truth to her husband, she would not respond to Aurelius as she does- "Than wol I love yow best of any man / Have heer my trouthe in al that evere I can" (326). The last few words imply that truth in marriage is all but impossible for its promisors to uphold. Dorigen's conflicting words "Ne shal I nevere been untrewe wfy" (312) reveal the inevitable failure of her pledge of faithfulness.

Once Arveragus discovers Dorigen's promise to Aurelius, his humble reaction reflects the state of imbalance in the marriage. The ridiculous length with which Arveragus goes to maintain his adherence to the idea that "[t]routhe is the hyest thing that man may kepe" (807) is incompatible with the behavior of a man deeply in love. Although their marital vows provide grounds for Dorigen to avoid fulfillment of her promise, he releases her to commit adultery "with glade chere in freendly wyse' (795). His response seem highly inappropriate, perhaps there is a pun on the word fiendish, considering that he values the pledge of truth to an outsider who plots to sabotage the preexisting truth in the relationship with his wife. He values the societal maintenance of truth to such an extreme degree that he would rather "dye in sorwe and in distresse" (924) than allow his wife to tarnish her commitment to truth less it be a reflection upon him. Concurrently, he treats truth hypocritically by forbidding Dorigen upon the "peyne of deeth" (809) of telling anyone of this affair. There lies a contradiction in his pledge to kill her if she threatens his honor while he concurrently allows himself to be cuckolded which is also a peril to his honor. Explaining this discrepancy could be the possibility that he dispatches her as a demonstration of his "maistre" (75) over her actions- the one condition that eliminates the possibility of love. The tears could be either a melodramatic attempt to feign his concern for her well being or a realization that he sacrifices a bit of honor in gaining dominance in the relationship.

Marriage becomes a conduit for men to display their "grete gentillesse" (851) instead of a union of lovers. After Dorigen's careless promise to Aurelius, she becomes a pawn in the high stake display of chivalric behavior. The concerns with rank emerges as a challenge of gallantry and honor which forces the knight, squire, and the philosopher to release each other from their truths. The fact that they are so willing to part with their pledges demonstrates the value placed upon words is directly tied to how it reflects upon social standing. The virtue of generosity becomes so entangled with the self-interests that no one commits acts of good will without ulterior motives of personal gain, framing this irony is the Franklin's question "Which was the moste free, as thnketh yowe?" (950). If a world places a higher position on truth in external interaction than it grants to private relationships, true love in the courtly tradition of behavior targeted to further self interest can never survive. In the tale's conclusion, Dorigen and Arveragus place the masks they wear when facing the outside world and reunite in a farce of mutually contentment. Perhaps "never eft ne was there angre hem bitwene" (881) although the wording suggests likewise, but even assuming that there is no discord, there appears to be no passionate love either.

Essay: On Cuckoldry: Women, Silence, and Subjectivity in the Merchant's Tale and the Manciple's Tale

by Eddie Borey
May 31, 2000

The Wife of Bath's extraordinary prologue gives the reader a dose of what is sometimes missing in early male-written literature: glimpses of female subjectivity. Women in medieval literature are often silent and passive, to the extent that cuckolding is often seen as something one man (the adulterer) does to another (the husband). Eve Sedgwick argues in Between Men that in many literary representations, women are playing pieces or playing fields in struggles between male players. By default it seems, male writers cannot help but create shallow constructions of women; heroism occurs in male spheres of activity, while the wives and daughters make the background, and the female love interest becomes a trophy. Unfortunately, when women are not silent they are often monsters and quite often, the silent ones conceal hidden dangers. Why should women present such a threat? Why do so many pre-modern (and, unfortunately, modern) male writers approach female subjects with such trepidation, with strategies of demonization or avoidance? Analysis of the Merchant's Tale and the Manciple's Tale proves fruitful in exploring these questions. In the sphere of the written word, women have often been silent in the West; the small number of great female medieval writers combined with a value system that praises passivity and quiet in their sex has effectively muffled female subjectivity, and yet somehow in silencing women men have doomed themselves to uneasiness and fear. To silence someone is to cut off access to her subjectivity, and in an intimate world like marriage such a formidable barrier quickly becomes a source of apprehension; woman becomes the terrifying, the unknown, the thing that betrays. The fear of cuckoldry presents a site where many of these issues of anxiety, silence, and subjectivity converge. Fear of cuckoldry is the unavoidable price of males ignoring or denying female voices. The inaccessibility of female subjectivity, caused by a male-imposed silence (imposed by both male characters and the male poet) paradoxically becomes a great source of anxiety for men; female characters become permeated by an aura of secrecy and mystery and simultaneously become treacherous and threatening to male order.

The reader catches only glimpses of May's innermost thoughts in the Merchant's Tale; January's inner desires and hopes are foregrounded. A third of the tale goes by before May even makes her first appearance, and even then the narrator keeps her at a distance. Initially, the reader knows nothing of her wishes or her desires in her marriage, although the narrator does inform us that "she was feffed in his lond" (l. 1698). The material benefits of the marriage seem a likely motivation, as January is both very old and very rich, but the reader has no direct access to May's thoughts. At the wedding, May continues to be an enigma. She is described in terms imbued with fantasy and mystery:

Mayus, that sit with so benyngne a chiere,

Hire to biholde it semed fayerye.

Queen Ester looked nevere with swich an ye

On Assuer, so meke a ook hath she. (ll. 1742-5)

To describe May as enchanting, Chaucer uses the word "fayerye," which also means fairy. She becomes a creature of fairy tales, described by a word that refers to something fantastic, unreal. The text also compares her favorably to Queen Esther, assuring the reader that Esther never looked on her king with such an eye. The choice of Esther as a point of reference is telling; Esther's beauty is not necessarily what readers of the Bible remember most about her. Queen Esther was a woman of secrets; she hid her Jewish heritage from the King, her husband. In likening May to Esther, the narrator seems to remind the reader of how little the text is really saying about May. The final simile that describes May's beauty in this passage is more memorable for how little it tells than for any poetic acuteness.

I may yow nat devyse al hir beautee;

But thus muche of hire beautee telle I may,

That she was lyk the brighte morwe of May,

Fulfild of alle beautee and pleasaunce. (ll. 1746-9)

The narrator begins with a disclaimer, saying that even her surface appearance must remain inaccessible to those reading the tale. This disclaimer is followed by an amazingly unhelpful simile: May is like the morrow of May. The element of cliché is not the only problem with the simile. Especially in a literary context, the reference to the month is already contained in May's own name. The simile becomes sadistically repetitive. In text, the word "May" (the name of the woman) becomes not only the signified but the signifier; her own name, in a way, calls us to liken her to the month. Consequently, the line likening her to the month shoves one metaphor back into itself, and then this simile becomes not one of A=B but rather A=A or even A within A. If a simile's two parts are too similar, then the simile ceases to be a simile, thus losing its poetic power to describe. Chaucer drives the point home by rhyming "May" with "may," setting up a parallel situation between his simile and his rhyme; "may" cannot properly be said to rhyme with "May" they are homophones. So in describing May on the night of the wedding feast, Chaucer first creates an aura of mystery, then intimates that much may be unknown about the bride, then finally gives the reader completely undescriptive lines about May's appearance.

The inaccessibility of her interior is a near-constant feature throughout the story. May almost never speaks and the first time the text directly renders her words, she is lying. (ll. 2188-2206). She opens her mouth for the first time with a long-winded speech assuring January of her own virtue. In fact, every time May speaks out loud in the tale, she lies. Her true intentions must be communicated to the reader through gestures, actions, and the narrator's very limited access to her thoughts. When May squeezes Damien's hand, her intentions become clear to both Damien and the reader (Pearsall 4/7). May's action of sleeping with Damien, of course, makes it fairly clearly what she wants. And her own thoughts, in a few limited glimpses, give the reader an imperfect portrait of what kind of woman May is. Her pity for Damien is the first (and last) twinge of emotion that could be called gentle:

"Certyn," thoghte she, "whom that this thyng displese,

I rekke noght, for heere I hym assure

To love hym best of any creature,

Though he namoore hadde than his sherte." (ll. 1982-5)

Here, the reader hears May's interior monologue for the first time. Of course, the moment is not terribly flattering for women. The narrator goes on to praise the soft-heartedness of women; of course, this soft-heartedness must be understood ironically in the context of adultery.

And, in a very real way, the reader can never quite know what May is about. She lets her wishes be known to Damien in a letter that the reader is never allowed to read (ll. 1996-7), and somehow this moment seems to encapsulate the reader's relationship with May's sexuality. The first great glimpse of her subjectivity comes in the wedding night bedroom scene, in which Chaucer sets up an incredible disparity between the experiences of January and May (Pearsall 4/7). We see January toiling and prancing about, revelling in his own love-making, while May keeps her own rather negative appraisal of his performance (musical and sexual) to herself: "She preyseth nat his pleyyng worth a bene" (l. 1854). Equally remarkable is the mindset with which January goes into the night:

But in his hearte he gan hire to manace

That he that nyght in armes wolde hire streyne

Harder than evere Parys dide Eleyne.

But natheless yet hadde he greet pitee

That thilke nyght offenden hire moste he

And thoughte, "Allas! O tendre creature,

Now wolde God ye myghte wel endure

Al my corage, it is so sharp and keene!" (ll. 1752-9)

To a modern reader especially, January's attitude toward the wedding night is sickening. She must submit; in a way, January accounts for her subjectivity in his pity for her, but he does not consider the possibility of her sexual agency. The language is one of conquest: in his heart he begins to "manace" her, and allusions to Paris and Helen conjure up a whole world of violence, abduction, war. His only consideration of her feelings is a hope that she will physically be able to endure him; the possibility of her sexual experience of pleasure and/or desire does not seem to occur to him. And yet her appraisal of his love-making that night would seem to suggest experience (Pearsall 4/7). While there is no anxiety on January's part, the reader and the narrator, with their total access to January's thoughts and limited glimpses of May's subjectivity, experiences plenty of anxiety. January's wishes to "manace" her seem sickening perhaps, but May's sheer inaccessibility makes her threatening in her own way. At play, in part, is a difference between the mechanics of male and female genitals. The reader always knows exactly what January is thinking; and, likewise, in bed it is never difficult to know what is on a man's mind. His genitals betray him; his pleasure and desire become totally legible. A woman's pleasure and desire are known to her and her alone. This disparity mirrors the disparity of knowledge in pregnancy: a woman always knows the baby is hers, and quite often can say for certain who fathered the child, but a man can never be quite sure. This inability to know what a woman enjoys in bed works itself out playfully in a rather coy omission of the narrator's:

And she obeyeth, be hire lief or looth.

But lest that precious folk be with me wrooth,

How that he wroghte, I dar nat to yow telle;

Of wheither hire thought it paradys or helle. (ll. 1961-4)

Quite simply, this passage is breathtaking. The narrator is playing with exactly those tensions between knowledge, silence, and subjectivity that underpin the terror of cuckoldry. He cannot tell us what she thinks because his audience does not want to hear about it; but, of course, we do wish to know, even if that knowledge is unsettling to us. January's confidence is, for the audience, what makes him so pitiable and, for men especially, what makes us unsure of ourselves. She is silenced, according to the narrator, in deference to a value system that (in the name of decency or other supposed virtues) seeks to deny female sexuality, but in silencing her the men doom themselves to uncertainty.

The Manciple's Tale deals directly with these tensions between uncertainty, silence, and subjectivity. Like the Merchant's Tale, the Manciple's Tale also (arguably) deals with a triangle of two men and one woman although one of the men, in this case, is a bird. Phoebus and his crow can be read as good friends. Phoebus has taught the bird how to speak, and the bird is unfailingly loyal. But there is also a way that the bird becomes fantasy or a symbol of representation itself:

Now hadde this Phebus in his hous a crowe

Which in a cage, he fostred many a day,

And taughte it speken, as men teche a jay.

Whit was this crowe as is a snow-whit swan,

And countrefete the speche of every man

He koude whan he sholde tell a tale. (ll. 130-5)

This bird exists nowhere in reality (section, 4/22). He is a crow with white feathers, a crow who can speak. Like a lie or language that misses the mark, the crow does not refer to anything real. Significantly, he can "counterfete" speech especially the speech of tale-tellers. The bird's language is tied to the act of story-telling itself, and is also described as mere mimicry or imitation.

And yet this bird is the mediator between Phoebus and knowledge of his wife. From the bird, Phoebus hears the news of his wife's adultery: "The crowe anon hym tolde, / By sadde tokenes and by wordes bolde, / How that his wyf had doon her lecherye" (ll. 257-9). The text dwells on the fact that the crow must use words and signs to communicate with his master "By sadde tokenes and by wordes bolde." Incongruent combinations dwell in this line (similar to the combination represented by the crow itself), and yet these combinations of sad signs and bold words are necessary to tell Phoebus the truth. Sadness and boldness, signs and words the use of difficult combinations makes the act of telling Phoebus into a kind of necessary but difficult performance. Phoebus consequently seems distanced from the actual act of adultery. She does not speak for herself the words that constitute the news come in a strange performance from a fantastic bird.

Phoebus's wife and her subjectivity are locked away from both Phoebus and the reader. She is completely and maddeningly silent. She does not utter a single word in the entire tale, nor does she have a name. Her judgment and execution are quick, efficient, final:

This Phebus gan awyward for to wryen,

And thoughte his sorweful herte brast atwo.

His bowe he bente, and sette therinne a flor,

And in his ire his wyf thanne hath he slayn. (ll. 262-5)

Phoebus begins his decent by turning away (from the truth? from facing the wife himself?) and slays her without giving her a chance to defend herself. Silencing her seems at first merciful for his own feelings, but this silence only causes more anguish and suffering. Once she is dead, he re-imagines her as faithful and curses the crow and the crow's descendents, making the bird the second victim of his violent temper (ll. 295-6). Her silence, Phoebus's protective measure for himself, becomes a source of great fear and anxiety. Uncertainty proves to be the terrible cost of making her subjectivity inaccessible; Phoebus's initial fear of cuckoldry, the motivation behind his wish to keep her under guard (l. 144), inverts and becomes a fear that she may have been faithful. The two male characters of the story both become victims of Phoebus's inability to know his wife.

The inaccessibility of female subjectivity, heightened by a male-imposed silence paradoxically becomes a terrifying source of male anxiety; female characters become imbued with an aura of mystery and simultaneously become treacherous and threatening to male order. The tensions in these stories and the male apprehensions clustered around the act of cuckoldry seem to draw intensity from a conviction that somehow both knowledge and ignorance are dangerous. Silencing women, while it certainly disempowers them, also seems in a way to disempower men. Even in the act of creating literature, in which a narrator presumably has unlimited power to create worlds and subjectivities, Chaucer seems at times to be reticent when it comes to the minds of his women perhaps that is why the Wife of Bath remains such a fascinating and exceptional character. Many of the tales center on the exploits of men, but women function as indispensable characters in the exploration of certain apprehensions and attitudes toward knowledge and ignorance. For male characters and the audience, the women of the Canterbury Tales, even when passive and silent, are often the sources of our most enthralled fascination and our most unsettling fears.

Quiz 1

1. **What is the first Canterbury Tale?**
    A. The Reeve's Tale
    B. The Knight's Tale
    C. The Miller's Tale
    D. The Cook's Tale

2. **Which tale in the first fragment seems to be unfinished?**
    A. The Reeve's Tale
    B. The Miller's Tale
    C. The Knight's Tale
    D. The Cook's Tale

3. **Which tale tells the story of Symkyn the miller?**
    A. The Reeve's Tale
    B. The Miller's Tale
    C. The Shipman's Tale
    D. The Wife of Bath's Tale

4. **Which characters are in love with Alison in the Miller's Tale?**
    A. Gervase and Nicholas
    B. Absolon and Nicholas
    C. John, Absolon and Nicholas
    D. Absolon and Gervase

5. **What is the name of the carpenter in the Miller's Tale?**
    A. Absolon
    B. Nicholas
    C. Fred
    D. John

6. **Who farts in Absolon's face?**
    A. Alison
    B. Gervase
    C. Nicholas
    D. John

7. **Who cries out "Water" because their arse has been branded with a hot iron?**
   A. Alison
   B. Absolon
   C. Nicholas
   D. John

8. **What is the genre of tales to which the Miller's Tale might belong?**
   A. romance
   B. modernist narrative
   C. fabliaux
   D. prose poem

9. **Which two characters are thought to be indistinguishable from each other in the Knight's Tale?**
   A. Theseus and Hippolyta
   B. Arcite and Palamon
   C. Arcite and Theseus
   D. Theseus and Palamon

10. **Who dies at the end of the Knight's Tale?**
    A. Arcite
    B. Palamon
    C. Theseus
    D. Hippolyta

11. **Who are Arcite and Palamon in love with?**
    A. Emelye
    B. Absolon
    C. Theseus
    D. Each other

12. **How many husbands has the Wife of Bath had?**
    A. 2
    B. 3
    C. 4
    D. 5

13. The Wife of Bath's first name is...

A. Alison

B. Absolon

C. She isn't given a first name, just "the Wife"

D. Bertha

14. The Wife of Bath's fifth husband is named...

A. Jankin

B. Absolon

C. January

D. Theseus

15. The Wife of Bath suffers, a little, from which ailment...

A. leprosy

B. deafness

C. muteness

D. blindness

16. What does the Wife use as a bargaining tool?

A. Sex

B. Food

C. Sleep

D. Money

17. The Wife of Bath claims to hate...

A. clerks and glossing

B. eating

C. cattle

D. men

18. In the General Prologue, which character is swathed in ten pounds of cloth?

A. The Wife of Bath

B. The Reeve

C. The Miller

D. The Summoner

19. **Which two characters are sometimes read as a homosexual couple?**
    A. Chaucer and the Reeve
    B. The Summoner and the Pardoner
    C. The Miller and the Reeve
    D. The Friar and the Summoner

20. **Chaucer is...**
    A. an imaginary character in the pilgrimage
    B. not mentioned within the text of the Tales
    C. a character in the pilgrimage, and the author of the work as a whole
    D. not the writer of the Canterbury Tales

21. **Which pilgrim throws a book into the fire?**
    A. The Wife of Bath
    B. The Reeve
    C. The Miller
    D. The Shipman

22. **What does the Man of Law refuse to tell a tale about?**
    A. incest
    B. murder
    C. blackmail
    D. Christians

23. **Who interrupts the Parson just before he is to tell his tale?**
    A. The Reeve
    B. The Shipman
    C. The Manciple
    D. The Summoner

24. **The Cook's real name is**
    A. Geoffrey Chaucer
    B. Roger of Ware
    C. Roger Warren
    D. Harry Bailly

25. **The Host's name is**
    A. Geoffrey Chaucer
    B. Harry Bailey
    C. Roger of Ware
    D. Roger Warren

Quiz 1 Answer Key

1. **(B)** The Knight's Tale
2. **(D)** The Cook's Tale
3. **(A)** The Reeve's Tale
4. **(C)** John, Absolon and Nicholas
5. **(D)** John
6. **(C)** Nicholas
7. **(C)** Nicholas
8. **(C)** fabliaux
9. **(B)** Arcite and Palamon
10. **(A)** Arcite
11. **(A)** Emelye
12. **(D)** 5
13. **(A)** Alison
14. **(A)** Jankin
15. **(B)** deafness
16. **(A)** Sex
17. **(A)** clerks and glossing
18. **(A)** The Wife of Bath
19. **(B)** The Summoner and the Pardoner
20. **(C)** a character in the pilgrimage, and the author of the work as a whole
21. **(A)** The Wife of Bath
22. **(A)** incest
23. **(B)** The Shipman
24. **(B)** Roger of Ware
25. **(B)** Harry Bailey

Quiz 2

1. **The Host prefers**
   A. not to hear tales at all
   B. lower-class characters to tell tales
   C. upper-class and high-status characters to tell tales
   D. women to tell tales

2. **The tale-telling game is thought up by which pilgrim?**
   A. The Wife of Bath
   B. The Host
   C. The Reeve
   D. The Manciple

3. **In which tale are friars said to live in Satan's arse in hell?**
   A. The Friar's Tale
   B. The Prioress' Tale
   C. The Summoner's Tale
   D. The Second Nun's Tale

4. **Constance appears in which tale?**
   A. The Nun's Priest's Tale
   B. The Reeve's Tale
   C. The Man of Law's Tale
   D. The Manciple's Tale

5. **The Man of Law's Tale focuses initially on which country?**
   A. England
   B. Siberia
   C. Scotland
   D. Syria

6. **Which character floats from location to location on a boat?**
   A. The Wife of Bath
   B. Theseus
   C. Griselda
   D. Constance

7. **What does Thomas give the friar in the Summoner's Tale?**
   A. a farthing
   B. some money
   C. some food and money
   D. a fart

8. **The friar in the Summoner's Tale gives a lengthy speech against...**
   A. sadness
   B. poverty
   C. death
   D. anger

9. **The question the knight in the Wife of Bath's tale has to answer to save his life is...**
   A. Why did you rape that maiden?
   B. Why do you wear that silly hat?
   C. Is Arcite or Palamon in the worse situation?
   D. What is it that women most desire?

10. **According to the Wife of Bath's Tale, women most desire**
    A. nice clothes to wear
    B. maistrie in marriage
    C. farting
    D. sex with their husbands

11. **What does Symkyn the miller do to distract the clerks from their corn?**
    A. Sets their horse free
    B. Cries out "Water!"
    C. Undresses his daughter
    D. Does a dance

12. **Why does John the carpenter hide in the roof in a kneading trough?**
    A. Because he believes Noah's flood is coming
    B. Because he is afraid of heights
    C. Because he is afraid of Nicholas
    D. Because he has murdered his wife

13. **Which pilgrim has a reputation for letting gravy out of pies?**
    A. The Cook
    B. The Reeve
    C. The Manciple
    D. The Summoner

14. **Who tells a tale which is explicitly anti-semitic?**
    A. The Reeve
    B. The Summoner
    C. The Prioress
    D. The Second Nun

15. **Who tells the tale of Chaunticleer and Pertelote?**
    A. The Monk
    B. The First Nun
    C. The Prioress
    D. The Second Nun

16. **Whose tale is a long recital of tragedies?**
    A. The Wife of Bath
    B. The Monk
    C. The Manciple
    D. The Merchant

17. **Who tells the tale of January and May?**
    A. The Monk
    B. The Miller
    C. The Manciple
    D. The Merchant

18. **Which tale was told to its teller by a merchant?**
    A. The Merchant's
    B. The Wife of Bath's
    C. The Shipman's
    D. The Man of Law's

19. **Who struggles to think of a tale to tell, because he says Chaucer has already told them all?**
    A. The Monk
    B. The Parson
    C. The Shipman
    D. The Man of Law

20. **What color does the devil dress in in the Friar's Tale?**
    A. Red
    B. Blue
    C. Black
    D. Green

21. **What happens to the summoner at the end of the Friar's Tale?**
    A. He is farted at
    B. Nothing - he gets away with it
    C. He is carried off to hell
    D. He dies

22. **Who quits the Friar's Tale?**
    A. The Monk
    B. The Reeve
    C. The Parson
    D. The Summoner

23. **Which tale that Chaucer tells is interrupted by the Host?**
    A. Melibee
    B. The Reeve's Tale
    C. The Knight's Tale
    D. Sir Thopas

24. **Who is the only pilgrim other than Chaucer to have literary ambitions?**
    A. The Wife of Bath
    B. The Squire
    C. The Manciple
    D. The Prioress

25. Which tale is written in rime royale?

    A. The Wife of Bath's

    B. The Reeve's

    C. The Miller's

    D. The Man of Law's

Quiz 2 Answer Key

1. **(C)** upper-class and high-status characters to tell tales
2. **(B)** The Host
3. **(C)** The Summoner's Tale
4. **(C)** The Man of Law's Tale
5. **(D)** Syria
6. **(D)** Constance
7. **(D)** a fart
8. **(D)** anger
9. **(D)** What is it that women most desire?
10. **(B)** maistrie in marriage
11. **(A)** Sets their horse free
12. **(A)** Because he believes Noah's flood is coming
13. **(A)** The Cook
14. **(C)** The Prioress
15. **(D)** The Second Nun
16. **(B)** The Monk
17. **(D)** The Merchant
18. **(D)** The Man of Law's
19. **(D)** The Man of Law
20. **(D)** Green
21. **(C)** He is carried off to hell
22. **(D)** The Summoner
23. **(D)** Sir Thopas
24. **(B)** The Squire
25. **(D)** The Man of Law's

Quiz 3

1. **"Quitting" is**
   A. farting
   B. hitting somebody in the face
   C. stopping, and giving up
   D. a revenge, response or repayment

2. **Which pair of words means "serious" and "fun"?**
   A. "ire" and "delite"
   B. "maistrie" and "sovereigntee"
   C. "Game" and "ernest"
   D. "gentilesse" and "stryvyng"

3. **Chaucer was famous in his lifetime as...**
   A. a singer
   B. a writer
   C. a civil servant
   D. a poet

4. **Chaucer's English is known today as**
   A. Middle English
   B. Pidgeon English
   C. End English
   D. Beginning English

5. **Chaucer's English has many words from**
   A. German
   B. many other languages, including French and Latin
   C. Spanish
   D. Japanese

6. **Who cries "Tehee!" after having her arse kissed by Absolon?**
   A. Emelye
   B. Alison
   C. The Wife of Bath
   D. The Prioress

7. **Chaunticleer's wife is**
    A. Alison
    B. Pertelote
    C. Emily
    D. Pamela

8. **Which tale ends by asking who was the most "fre"?**
    A. The Reeve's Tale
    B. The Miller's Tale
    C. The Shipman's Tale
    D. The Franklin's Tale

9. **Who sets out to "quit" the Miller?**
    A. The Reeve
    B. The Parson
    C. The Plowman
    D. The Pardoner

10. **Who tells the tale about Canacee?**
    A. Chaucer
    B. The Squire
    C. Francis Petrarch
    D. The Man of Law

11. **What is significant about Griselde's clothing?**
    A. It seems to define her personality
    B. It disappears when she clicks her fingers
    C. It is always green
    D. She made it herself

12. **January marries a young wife named...**
    A. August
    B. May
    C. June
    D. July

13. **What does the wife in The Shipman's Tale realize that she can sell?**
    A. Her hair
    B. Her food
    C. Her body
    D. Her time

14. **How many Alisons appear in the Tales?**
    A. 1 (The Wife of Bath)
    B. 3 (The Wife of Bath, John's wife in The Miller's Tale, and the Wife of Bath's friend)
    C. 4 (The Wife of Bath, John's wife in The Miller's Tale, the Emperor's daughter in the Man of Law's Tale, and the Wife of Bath's friend)
    D. 2 (The Wife of Bath and John's wife in The Miller's Tale)

15. **Whose tale tells of the brutal sacrifice of Virginius' daughter?**
    A. The Pardoner's
    B. The Physician's
    C. The Monk's
    D. The Prioress'

16. **Which adjective usually describes Nicholas in the Miller's Tale?**
    A. crafte (crafty)
    B. large (tall)
    C. hende (handy)
    D. yonge (young)

17. **What sort of tree do Damien and May have sex in in the Merchant's Tale?**
    A. a horse-chesnut tree
    B. a pear tree
    C. an oak
    D. an apple tree

18. **Which character in the Merchant's Tale goes blind?**
    A. January
    B. Justinus
    C. May
    D. Damien

19. **Which god and goddess pair appears in the Merchant's Tale?**
   A. Pluto and Proserpina
   B. Mars and Apollo
   C. Juno and Jupiter
   D. Echo and Narcissus

20. **What material is the horse made out of in the Squire's Tale?**
   A. silver
   B. gold
   C. cloth
   D. brass

21. **What is important about cloth in the Tales?**
   A. It burns very easily
   B. "Text" and "textile" are closely linked
   C. It's not worth very much
   D. "Cloth" and "closed" are related concepts

22. **What do the three fools seek in the Pardoner's Tale?**
   A. Life
   B. Food
   C. Death
   D. Water

23. **Which pilgrim is potentially a eunuch?**
   A. The Wife of Bath
   B. The Knight
   C. The Shipman
   D. The Pardoner

24. **Which pilgrim is a lawyer?**
   A. The Wife of Bath
   B. The Knight
   C. The Man of Law
   D. The Pardoner

25. **What is the evil judge called in the Physician's Tale?**
    A. Appius
    B. Apollius
    C. Virginius
    D. Titus Livius

Quiz 3 Answer Key

1. **(D)** a revenge, response or repayment
2. **(C)** "Game" and "ernest"
3. **(C)** a civil servant
4. **(A)** Middle English
5. **(B)** many other languages, including French and Latin
6. **(B)** Alison
7. **(B)** Pertelote
8. **(D)** The Franklin's Tale
9. **(A)** The Reeve
10. **(B)** The Squire
11. **(A)** It seems to define her personality
12. **(B)** May
13. **(C)** Her body
14. **(B)** 3 (The Wife of Bath, John's wife in The Miller's Tale, and the Wife of Bath's friend)
15. **(B)** The Physician's
16. **(C)** hende (handy)
17. **(B)** a pear tree
18. **(A)** January
19. **(A)** Pluto and Proserpina
20. **(D)** brass
21. **(B)** "Text" and "textile" are closely linked
22. **(C)** Death
23. **(D)** The Pardoner
24. **(C)** The Man of Law
25. **(A)** Appius

Quiz 4

1. **Who are January's two advisors in the Merchant's Tale?**
   A. Justinus and Placebo
   B. Apollo and Ariadne
   C. Morecambe and Wise
   D. Damian and May

2. **What happens when Griselde is reunited with her children ?**
   A. She does not recognise them
   B. She will not release them from her embrace
   C. She dies
   D. She murders them

3. **Who does Griselde marry?**
   A. Walter
   B. The Clerk
   C. Apaulinus
   D. The Merchant

4. **Which pilgrim's tale is interrupted courteously by the Franklin?**
   A. The Wife of Bath
   B. The Squire
   C. The Shipman
   D. The Prioress

5. **Who interrupts Chaucer's tale of Sir Thopas?**
   A. The Monk
   B. The Host
   C. The Knight
   D. The Franklin

6. **Which quarrel, later a "quitting" match, starts up during the Wife of Bath's tale?**
   A. The quarrel between the Miller and the Reeve
   B. The quarrel between the Prioress and the Wife of Bath
   C. The quarrel between the Knight and the Squire
   D. The quarrel between the Friar and the Summoner

7. **Which pilgrim is the Knight's son?**
   A. The Squire
   B. The Shipman
   C. The Pardoner
   D. The Summoner

8. **Which pilgrim eats delicately and courteously at the table, not allowing a morsel to fall onto their breast?**
   A. The Wife of Bath
   B. The Knight
   C. The Shipman
   D. The Prioress

9. **Who, in the Manciple's Tale, silences the crow?**
   A. Pallas
   B. Phebus
   C. Apollo
   D. Jupiter

10. **What color does the crow in the Manciple's Tale start off as - and what is he by the end?**
    A. White, turned to black.
    B. Black, turned to white.
    C. Yellow, turned to orange.
    D. Red, turned to green.

11. **What message might be inferred from both the Manciple's and the Nun's Priest's Tales?**
    A. Keep your mouth shut
    B. Use your body as a business tool
    C. Forsake sin
    D. Preserve your virginity

12. **What does the Wife of Bath argue about her "bele chose"?**
    A. If men see it as profitable, why shouldn't she be the one to profit?
    B. Her husband should be the one to profit from it's use
    C. She should use it only once a week
    D. It shouldn't be used

13. **What is the Wife of Bath's "bele chose"?**
    A. Her face
    B. Her money
    C. Her clothes
    D. Her "queynte"

14. **Which religious festival does the ending of the Summoner's Tale parody?**
    A. Easter
    B. The Pentecost
    C. The Crucifixion
    D. Christmas

15. **How is the rapacious friar in the Summoner's Tale repaid?**
    A. By being branded
    B. With a fart
    C. With a burp
    D. With one thousand franks

16. **What is the sum the monk borrows in the Shipman's Tale?**
    A. 100 franks
    B. 200 franks
    C. 100 pounds
    D. 200 pounds

17. **Who do scholars think was originally to tell the tale which we now think of as the Shipman's?**
    A. The Wife of Bath
    B. The Franklin
    C. The Pardoner
    D. The Summoner

18. **What explanation does the Man of Law's tale give for how Constance survives?**
    A. The grace of God
    B. Extra food hidden in the soles of her shoes
    C. Food parcels dropped by birds
    D. Using up body fat

19. **What is the final line of the Cook's Tale as we have it?**
    A. a wife, who kept a shop
    B. a wife, who had sex for a living
    C. a cook, who baked excellent pies
    D. a husband, who had murdered three people

20. **What happens at the end of the Cook's Tale?**
    A. A happy ending
    B. Everyone dies
    C. A bittersweet ending
    D. It's unfinished - we don't precisely know

21. **Who debatably comes off best in the Shipman's Tale?**
    A. The wife
    B. The monk
    C. The squire
    D. The merchant

22. **Who claims that they will never tell a tale about incest?**
    A. The Reeve
    B. The Man of Law (and Chaucer)
    C. The Miller
    D. The Shipman

23. **What might be said to be the theme of the Pardoner's tale?**
    A. Homosexuals should be equal to heterosexuals
    B. Women should be equal to men
    C. Money is the root of all evil
    D. Credit is excellent

24. **What is the final tale told?**
    A. The Parson's Tale
    B. The Shipman's Tale
    C. The Pardoner's Tale
    D. The Summoner's Tale

25. **For what reason does the Retraction retract the Tales?**
    A. Because they are incomplete
    B. Because they are potentially sinful
    C. Because they are too overtly religious
    D. Because they contain too much sexual material

Quiz 4 Answer Key

1. **(A)** Justinus and Placebo
2. **(B)** She will not release them from her embrace
3. **(A)** Walter
4. **(B)** The Squire
5. **(B)** The Host
6. **(D)** The quarrel between the Friar and the Summoner
7. **(A)** The Squire
8. **(D)** The Prioress
9. **(B)** Phebus
10. **(A)** White, turned to black.
11. **(A)** Keep your mouth shut
12. **(A)** If men see it as profitable, why shouldn't she be the one to profit?
13. **(D)** Her "queynte"
14. **(B)** The Pentecost
15. **(B)** With a fart
16. **(A)** 100 franks
17. **(A)** The Wife of Bath
18. **(A)** The grace of God
19. **(B)** a wife, who had sex for a living
20. **(D)** It's unfinished - we don't precisely know
21. **(A)** The wife
22. **(B)** The Man of Law (and Chaucer)
23. **(C)** Money is the root of all evil
24. **(A)** The Parson's Tale
25. **(B)** Because they are potentially sinful

ClassicNotes

GrAdeSaver™

Getting you the grade since 1999™

Other ClassicNotes from GradeSaver™

1984
Absalom, Absalom
Adam Bede
The Adventures of Augie
    March
The Adventures of
    Huckleberry Finn
The Adventures of Tom
    Sawyer
The Aeneid
Agamemnon
The Age of Innocence
The Alchemist (Coelho)
The Alchemist (Jonson)
Alice in Wonderland
All My Sons
All Quiet on the Western
    Front
All the King's Men
All the Pretty Horses
The Ambassadors
American Beauty
Angela's Ashes
Animal Farm
Anna Karenina
Antigone
Antony and Cleopatra
Aristotle's Ethics
Aristotle's Poetics
Aristotle's Politics
As I Lay Dying
As You Like It
Astrophil and Stella
The Awakening
Babbitt
The Bacchae

Bartleby the Scrivener
The Bean Trees
The Bell Jar
Beloved
Benito Cereno
Beowulf
Bhagavad-Gita
Billy Budd
Black Boy
Bleak House
Bless Me, Ultima
The Bloody Chamber
Bluest Eye
The Bonfire of the
    Vanities
The Book of the Duchess
    and Other Poems
Brave New World
Breakfast at Tiffany's
Breakfast of Champions
The Brothers Karamazov
The Burning Plain and
    Other Stories
A Burnt-Out Case
By Night in Chile
Call of the Wild
Candide
The Canterbury Tales
Cat on a Hot Tin Roof
Cat's Cradle
Catch-22
The Catcher in the Rye
The Caucasian Chalk
    Circle
The Cherry Orchard
The Chocolate War

The Chosen
A Christmas Carol
Christopher Marlowe's
    Poems
Chronicle of a Death
    Foretold
Civil Disobedience
Civilization and Its
    Discontents
A Clockwork Orange
The Color of Water
The Color Purple
Comedy of Errors
Communist Manifesto
A Confederacy of
    Dunces
Confessions
Connecticut Yankee in
    King Arthur's Court
The Consolation of
    Philosophy
Coriolanus
The Count of Monte
    Cristo
Crime and Punishment
The Crucible
Cry, the Beloved
    Country
The Crying of Lot 49
Cymbeline
Daisy Miller
Death in Venice
Death of a Salesman
The Death of Ivan Ilych
Democracy in America
Devil in a Blue Dress

For our full list of over 250 Study Guides, Quizzes,
Sample College Application Essays, Literature Essays and E-texts, visit:

www.gradesaver.com

ClassicNotes

GrAdeSaver™

Getting you the grade since 1999™

Other ClassicNotes from GradeSaver™

For our full list of over 250 Study Guides, Quizzes,
Sample College Application Essays, Literature Essays and E-texts, visit:

www.gradesaver.com

ClassicNotes

GrAdeSaver™

Getting you the grade since 1999™

Other ClassicNotes from GradeSaver™

The Love Song of J.
   Alfred Prufrock
Lucy
Macbeth
Madame Bovary
Manhattan Transfer
Mansfield Park
MAUS
The Mayor of
   Casterbridge
Measure for Measure
Medea
Merchant of Venice
Metamorphoses
The Metamorphosis
Middlemarch
Midsummer Night's
   Dream
Moby Dick
Moll Flanders
Mother Courage and Her
   Children
Mrs. Dalloway
Much Ado About
   Nothing
My Antonia
Mythology
Native Son
Night
Nine Stories
No Exit
Notes from Underground
O Pioneers
The Odyssey
Oedipus Rex or Oedipus
   the King

Of Mice and Men
The Old Man and the Sea
Oliver Twist
On Liberty
On the Road
One Day in the Life of
   Ivan Denisovich
One Flew Over the
   Cuckoo's Nest
One Hundred Years of
   Solitude
Oroonoko
Othello
Our Town
Pale Fire
Paradise Lost
A Passage to India
The Pearl
Persuasion
Phaedra
Phaedrus
The Picture of Dorian
   Gray
Poems of W.B. Yeats:
   The Rose
Poems of W.B. Yeats:
   The Tower
The Poisonwood Bible
Portrait of the Artist as a
   Young Man
Pride and Prejudice
The Prince
Prometheus Bound
Pudd'nhead Wilson
Pygmalion
Rabbit, Run

A Raisin in the Sun
The Real Life of
   Sebastian Knight
The Red Badge of
   Courage
The Remains of the Day
The Republic
Rhinoceros
Richard II
Richard III
The Rime of the Ancient
   Mariner
Robinson Crusoe
Roll of Thunder, Hear
   My Cry
Romeo and Juliet
A Room of One's Own
A Room With a View
Rosencrantz and
   Guildenstern Are
   Dead
Salome
The Scarlet Letter
The Scarlet Pimpernel
The Secret Life of Bees
Secret Sharer
Sense and Sensibility
A Separate Peace
Shakespeare's Sonnets
Shantaram
Siddhartha
Silas Marner
Sir Gawain and the
   Green Knight
Sister Carrie

For our full list of over 250 Study Guides, Quizzes,
Sample College Application Essays, Literature Essays and E-texts, visit:

www.gradesaver.com

ClassicNotes

GradeSaver™

Getting you the grade since 1999™

For our full list of over 250 Study Guides, Quizzes,
Sample College Application Essays, Literature Essays and E-texts, visit:

www.gradesaver.com

Made in the USA
Lexington, KY
30 September 2012